ANDREI CODRESCU POETRY COLLECTIONS

1970 *License to Carry a Gun*
1973 *A Serious Morning*
1973 *The History of the Growth of Heaven*
1975 *The Life & Times of An Involuntary Genius*
1977 *The Marriage of Insult and Injury*
1977 *The Lady Painter*
1978 *For the Love Of a Coat*
1980 *Necrocorrida*
1983 *Selected Poems 1970-1980*
1991 *Belligerence*
1996 *Alien Candor: Selected Poems, 1970-1995*
1997 *Comrade Past & Mister Present/Candoare Spräinä*
2000 *Selected Poetry/Poezii alese*
2003 *It Was Today: new poems*
2005 *Instrumentul negru: poezii 1965-1968*
2007 *Submarinul Iertat* (with Ruxandra Cesereanu)
2007 *Femeia neagrä a unui culcuș de hoți*
2009 *The Forgiven Submarine* (with Ruxandra Cesereanu)
2013 *So Recently Rent a World: New and Selected Poems*
2016 *Arta Uitării/The Art of Forgetting: new poems*
2017 *Submarinul Iertat anniversary edition* (with Ruxandra Cesereanu)
2019 *no time like now: new poems 2016-2018*
2019 *Metroul F*
2021 *Visul Diacritic*
2022 *too late for nightmares*

VINCENT KATZ POETRY COLLECTIONS

1978 *Rooms*
1986 *A Tremor In The Morning* (with Alex Katz)
1988 *Cabal Of Zealots*
1990 *New York Hello!* (with Rudy Burckhardt)
1993 *Acid*
1994 *Voyages* (with James Brown)
1997 *Boulevard Transportation* (with Rudy Burckhardt)
1998 *Pearl* (with Tabboo!)
2000 *Understanding Objects*
2005 *Rapid Departures* (with Mario Cafiero)
2007 *Judge* (with Wayne Gonzales)
2008 *Alcuni Telefonini* (with Francesco Clemente)
2008 *Berlin* (with Matthias Mansen)
2015 *Swimming Home*
2016 *Southness*
2017 *Fantastic Caryatids* (with Anne Waldman)
2020 *Broadway for Paul*
2021 *Previous Glances: an intense togetherness*

A Possible Epic of Care

A Collaborative Poem
by

Andrei Codrescu & Vincent Katz

BLACK
WIDOW
PRESS
BOSTON

Black Widow Press is an imprint of Commonwealth Books, Inc., Boston, MA. Distributed to the trade by NBN (National Book Network) throughout North America, Canada, and the U.K. Black Widow Press and its logo are registered trademarks of Commonwealth Books, Inc.

Joseph S. Phillips and Susan J. Wood, Ph.D., Publishers
www.blackwidowpress.com

Cover photograph: "Captiva Island #11 (2015)" by Vivien Bittencourt
Cover design & interior text production: Geoff Munsterman

ISBN-13: 979-8-9880852-2-5 (paperback)

Printed in the United States of America

SPECIAL THANKS

Andrei Codrescu is grateful to Lynnea Villanova, Eva Mantel, the Codrescu tribe, Yvonne and Oren Steinberger, Carmen Firan, Adrian Sângeorzan, Florea Firan, Alexandra Carides, Vivien Bittencourt, Radu Vancu, Cristina Vănoagă, Svetlana Cârstean, Anca Stuparu, John Godfrey, Greg Masters, Jeff Wright, Bob Holman, Ram Devinini, Elinor Nauen, Anne Waldman, Ruxandra Cesereanu, Corin Braga, Mihaela Moscaliuc, Michael Waters, Sharon Mesmer, David Borchardt, Dan Shafran, Justin Brice Guariglia, Jacques Sirvain, Ivan Suvanjieff, Dawn Engle, Roger Conover, Julian and Laura Semilian, Pat and Gail Nolan, Peter Maravelas, David Ross, Loren Fishman, Carol Ardman, Hugh Rogovy, Lulu Parent, Radu and Cristina Polizu, Ariel Dorfman, Ioana Avădani, Anselm and Eddie Berrigan, Valery and Ruth Oisteanu, Dave Mandl, Olivia Eaton, Willis Barnstone, Kim Stoddard, Pablos Holman, Linda Stone, Oana Havres, Nicolae Tzone, Peter Carlaftes, Kat Georges, the Virus, the Vaccine, the American Voters who vanquished Evil, and of course my ever-vigilant and well-versed dear collaborator, Vincent Katz.

Vincent Katz would like to thank Luisa Del Moro, Vincenzo Del Moro, Ada Katz, Alex Katz, Joe Phillips, Geoff Munsterman, Anne Waldman, Eleni Sikelianos, Caroline Swanson, Audrey Coombe, Rachel Levitsky, Trace Peterson, Eileen Myles, Elaine Equi, Jerome Sala, Lilian Tone, Joshua Decter, Lynnea Villanova, Isaac Katz, Oliver Katz, and Vivien Bittencourt for their significant contributions to this epic. And a special thank you to his partner in this collaboration, Andrei Codrescu.

A Possible Epic of Care was composed between February 4, 2020, and July 23, 2021

A Possible Epic
of Care

CANTO
UNO

The "diamond vehicle" : the practice of taking the result as the path

It's Mozart's birthday. He's only 264. How is it that we're getting older, while he stays young? Is that some magic of music? But we've got music too; we're not out of here yet.

He signed the "Dying Young" contract when he was writing the music for *Don Juan* in Prague with a girl on his lap and a chest of wine and cognac, half-empty bottles in reach of the piano. So says Giacomo Casanova, whose collaboration with Lorenzo da Ponte was a devil's bargain. Casanova was hired to write one of his true amorous adventures for the libretto that Da Ponte had trouble with because he had no experience with women. Casanova arranged for the girl to be positioned where she'd do the music best good, and filled Mozart with alcohol. Immortality is a bargain. Mozart signed. He'd have signed it even if he hadn't been drunk and aroused. Us, older geniuses, remember well that Mozart-moment when we could have signed that deal. We are not out of here, but where is Giacomo? Da Ponte lived to a ripe old age in New York teaching Italian to Park Avenue brats and going to silent bird bars. Mozart or Da Ponte? Heads or tails? Rimbaud or Soupault? Jarry or Queneau? O'Hara or Godfrey?

Frank Zappa stays young as well. Don't you dig "Transylvania Boogie"? Anything that takes us across the forests. Anything that takes us across anything.

I listen now and think, "What a Transylvania!" I was born in Sibiu, the Austro-Hungarian model city for moveable type one month after Gutenberg. Baron von Bruckenthal invented torture machines now on display at the Bruckenthal National Museum. There is a bit of a mechanic in all of us, as we say in Hollywood. And why are people dumping on bats? Bram Stoker tapped a vein. Bats are perfect carriers of synthesizable viruses. See today's newspaper. What do you carry, reader? What is your skill and your virus?

So I'm sitting here listening to *Chunga's Revenge* and looking at two magazine covers. I was walking on the avenue the other day when I spied one of those windows displaying an array of current mags, and I thought, how quaint! Magazines! Actual, physical products. They won't be around for long. And suddenly I longed for the magazine experience.

Gutenberg printed the Bible, it sold well, then a second book, on the horrors of Dracula and bats, and that was the world's first best seller. In Copacabana in 1993 I leafed through Brazilian *Vogue* to look at models, but then I saw that all the women on the beach were more beautiful. It was the last *Vogue* I saw, though the subject came up when I asked Mark Strand, who wrote for *Vogue*, if I might too. He said nothing. I think that Strawberry Saroyan works for *Vogue*. Strand is dead so there is a vacuum. I don't want to work there now. In my mail box await *Harper's, The New Yorker, Los Angeles Review of Books, The New York Review of Books, The Paris Review, Poetry Project Newsletter, Lapham's Quarterly,* and *Foreign Policy.* I would rather look at *Vogue* now. It's end of January 2020 in Brooklyn and print targets us. I wish I was Mozart.

Now I sit in a contemporary coffee chain reading two. From one, beam the faces of the top four Democratic candidates for president. Iowa is next week, and as my friend said yesterday at lunch, the priority is Orange Man Out. The reality is much more. On the cover of the other, one of the most beautiful women alive lounges, her almond skin bedecked in a few, delicate tattoos. Her eyes have a languid, distant look, imbued with a touch of sadness.

One must collage! It's an imperative, like the once dictum, "Get it used." The candidates, straw puppets of the new century, the 20s no less!, need to absorb the languor, skin, tattoos, and almonds of beauty. I have a long table I bought for this. One day Vincent Katz and Andrei Codrescu sit at this table with scissors and glue. It is still the 20s. Then they go to the cabaret to perform their collages before the police raid next morning.

One periodical is ostensibly about politics and culture, the other fashion, but they intersect. At the intersection of politics and culture, like at the intersection of Music and Humanity, two streets in New Orleans, stands a pimply high-school kid with a saxophone. The overpass of Interstate I-10 sends back sound to his delighted ears. Give that boy a contract.

My mother, 95 in Florida, thanked me the first day for bringing a message from "Andrei." I said, "I am Andrei." No dice. Next day, she saw me, "Andrei, you are here. Someone came yesterday with a message from you." I had the distinct impression that she liked "Andrei" better than Andrei.

You are writing about your mother, and I am writing about mine. We are writing about our mothers, who are both in their 90s. I took my mother to get her hair washed and cut. Traditionally, my father cut my mother's hair, which she washed herself, usually in the sink. When she'd finished washing it, she'd wrap a towel around it and flip it up so that it looked like a turban. It *was* a turban. I'm surprised he never painted her that way. It was such an iconic image to me as a kid. She looked elegant and simultaneously approachable.

After the haircut, we had lunch, then went to Dr. Hanna, who gave her a cortisone injection for the pain in her right knee. While there, she explained to the doctor and his assistant that I was her uncle, not her husband. Then she reiterated, she and I were brother and sister. Then we went to get a mani pedi in a place on 18th Street that played New Age music as the high school kids raged and laughed across the street.

* * *

Ted Berrigan looms over these poems
The Sonnets is a masterpiece of modern conviction
on the 15th day of November in the year of the motorcar
a subway filled with guilt ran off the track into history.

You can collaborate on the epic of life and take possible care of business
speak with affection of your mother
but you cannot exchange mothers no matter time or space
though age ruins them and us with methodical indifference.

In Venice at his grave I quoted Pound to himself:
"What matters in the end is the quality of affection"
a line dear to me but what the cranky old bastard wrote was:

"nothing matters but the quality of affection in the end,"
something quite different that begins with "nothing"
and ends with "the end."

* * *

Did Pound love his mother?
Maybe Olga Rudge, buried next to him, knew,
and answered if someone asked.

* * *

"All things are tragic when a mother watches," per Frank O'Hara.
They did and do, but they are unique and we cannot trade them like cities.
Trading New York for Tokyo, for instance, makes sense.
Everybody above the first floor, because we want our stores.

Mothers, cities, women in *Vogue*, and poets collaborating in New York.
What more can an epic be about than stories about how we care?
But no stories are suspenseful without war. So with such matters in our care
let us recall the wars that made us poets in the days when our mothers

were young in their respective cities, countries and continents.
Won't somebody take me out tonight?
The rest is dross. The email address of someone you care about.
Somebody will, but it will work like early Philip Glass

"To leave your house in New York now costs $30" – John Godfrey, 2019.
I first wrote 1919. We thank you Great Spirit that the Great War is over.

* * *

We love Wilfred Owen but hate the hangover!
We were seen right away by Céline
And now we have to wait and wait
Where is the doctor? Out on a limb no doubt

Jim Carroll *Organic Trains* more fruitful and more forthcoming
insofar as Jim was shy in Bolinas when Joanne Kyger was prying
that monkey off his back, and now that I think of it, all of us
walked around with monkeys' claws dug deep into our backs,

hoping Joanne would pry them off, and one time she saved my life
directly, even the monkey was grateful:
a guy in a two-seater sports convertible picked me up hitchhiking
on Hwy 1 from Monte Rio to Bolinas in 1975 or thereabouts

beautiful California day the Pacific 1,000 feet sparkling below the curves
of the road the driver took insanely not saying a word.

* * *

I was sure the impending plunge was a few seconds away,
which I noted, and said What's the rush?
I was going to kill myself driving into the ocean, he said,
but felt I should take someone with me.

And that someone, I said, is me? I'm a poet I have a few more poems
to write, including one with Vincent Katz in the second decade of the next
millennium, so if you let me off right here that would be great!
Right Here was about a foot on the crest of hill off the asphalt

below which the Pacific was licking its lips of gentle waves preparing for
    high tide,
but hell, I'd rather have an ocean over me than eternity in a sports car with
    this maniac.
Poet, he said. Bullshit! I'm a poet!
Well, yeah, you see, poets shouldn't kill themselves in company, I said,

they might have to read each other's poems forever on the other side.
What's your name? I said Andrei Codrescu.

* * *

Bullshit! he cried. Andrei Codrescu is this old beatnik who died a long
    time ago.
I had no ID or book on me I believed in having nothing in those days
— except the monkey on my back — so I said I'm him I can prove it I'm
    going
to a party in Bolinas at Joanne Kyger's all kind of poets will be there:
    Robert Creeley Jim Carroll
Lewis MacAdams Tom Clark Jim Gustafson Diane di Prima...
Bullshit, bullshit! Those are all old beatniks all dead I saw that book!
No, it's true!

* * *

And it was! When we got to Joanne's her yard was full of poets smoking, drinking beer, talking all at once. Joanne, elegant and breezy in a billowing white dress or scarf, stood regally on her second story porch looking with psilocybin eyes on the mass of swirling poets and at the Bay beyond, and when the guy who had decided to kill himself only if the poets he said were dead were indeed dead braked the roadster on the dirt road of her gate, Joanne took him in at once and saw him through his troubles. She drew him straight to her to work magic, and last I saw he was heading up the stairs. I fell ravenously on one of the Jims, who handed me a beer because I looked like I really needed one. That's the last I saw of the guy who didn't believe that I was alive, and who Joanne saved me from, and possibly him, though, in my opinion, there is no saving a poet who thinks all poets are dead. It is true that everyone in Joanne's yard that beautiful sparkly day in Bolinas is now dead, but I'm still alive and writing this story in our Epic of Care for Vincent who wrote "Jim Carroll..." and it all came back to me.

CANTO DOS

It is a Tuesday in early March. The bass throbs in Starbucks. It is somewhat impeding my enjoyment of *Agrippina*, which I am listening to on Spotify, in advance of our visit to the Met tonight. Joyce DiDonato sings the title role in the recording, and she will sing tonight.

I learned only recently, through a really cool TV series featuring violinist and conductor Scott Yoo, that Handel spent his formative years in Rome. He is usually identified with his life-changing success in London.

Joyce DiDonato is from Kansas City.

Agrippina is such a story for our time, and the music, and therefore the story, flows effortlessly. No wonder it was such a hit.
And this music, apart from anything in the story itself, is helping me understand my life.

I am a writer. See you in Oaxaca.

Our friends died last week in a crash in Mexico, where they lived. It is so strange.

* * *

How do you care for the dead?
Kaddish. *The Tibetan Book of the Dead.*
And then year after year Dia de los Muertos.
All Saints' Day in New Orleans.
My dead, you are watching, no?
Hard cars, soft bodies, broken hearts.
Jeffrey and Glenn died when the VW hit a tree
on the Russian River village of Monte Rio
in California in 1977 before the internet.
In our dead lies the secret of greatness.
Jeffrey is a great poet still. Ted Berrigan.
Jim Carroll. The real marketing machine
of the cosmos is poetry. The internet
is the shadow of an egret in the clear lake

of eternity, I mean music.
When Jeffrey died our common friend Hunce Voelcker
insisted on reading for forty days the Coleman translation
of the *Tibetan Book of the Dead* intro by Carl Jung
while I read the Chögyam Trungpa translation
simultaneously, choosing accuracy over beauty
in guiding the soul of our friend through the Bardo.
Coleman, Trungpa said, got a color wrong, meaning
that the soul might wander in the wrong direction
because of the mistranslation, reincarnating as a cockroach,
let's say, instead of the non-Jeffrey he might have escaped in.
I would rather Jeffrey got through the Bardo and did not reincarnate.
Hunce thought that being a cockroach is preferable to nothingness.
Hunce also believed that beauty is superior to accuracy.
He left his money to the American Poetry Academy for a poetry prize.
Hunce loved Hart Crane but I liked *Scientific American*.

* * *

WE ARE CURRENTLY, RIGHT NOW, IN 30 SECONDS OF
SILENCE REMEMBERING THE GREAT MCCOY TYNER, WHO
JUST PASSED AWAY

* * *

WKCR is speaking
and playing
"Message from the Nile"
from his album
Extensions
featuring
Elvin Jones
Wayne Shorter
Alice Coltrane
Gary Bartz
Ron Carter

* * *

Alice's harp is waving through my hair
weaving itself through McCoy's hand
through piano chords
rhythm pulsing almost like that great TV theme of yore
and now the horns come in in unison
they are praying as they slip
lightly and steadily over a horizon
dolphins jumping the spray of Alice's waves

now the piano is soloing
or rather explicating
the left hand anchoring
an ambitious outlay of rhythm in the right
the right and left
not different sides of the aisle
but one psyche interwoven

the psychic expansion of the music
as differences confronted
not on the street though
no, this extension exists in some beyond
some parallel that we visited
and could never return to
as Aeneas too could never return
the voyage only one consistent out

Wayne on soprano picks up the sail
he too flying the waves of piano push
Elvin hyperventilating below in chops

the harp is thrilling us again
with the breaths of life and mbira sound

*　*　*

(I saw McCoy live once
Solid)

*　*　*

silence
when the last note expires
in the room you're in
deep silence knowing
it will no more follow the fancies and secrets
of the live show that filled you with things
of the mind and images of reeds in dreams

the silence when the recording ends
is delighted to make the voyages start again
to thieves' markets where all the goods for sale
were stolen from you when you were gone

you return to the time
when the living promised more
but buy what they made when you were there
sublime trips to islands of youth

we all made some things that were more
than traces records books and others out of tune
anecdotes in promiscuous memories of art

I buy my own old books and wonder how they made such sound

Welcome the thieves

* * *

I like to go out in the morning because I like to see New Yorkers. I always say anyone who's lived in New York more than a month is a New Yorker. New Yorkers are survivors. This too they survive.

Thank god for Telemann. Western culture has never been a thing. Western power has been, and power likes certain kinds of culture, but look at mid last century Germany. Who won there? The official art, or the Degenerate Art? Artists operate on the periphery, always, and sometimes deep toward the center. Thank god for Charlie Watts.

The Grand Princess is moored at the Port of Oakland. Oliver flies back from Berkeley tonight. Isaac is here and may not return to finish his semester.

On the radio, Smetana's *Moldau* keeps flowing. It reminds me of another river — the Housatonic, as featured in Robert Underwood Johnson's poem, which Charles Ives set to song.

* * *

I'm almost able to write a poem, outside in this warm March weather, listening to the sounds of basketballs being bounced, swings creaking and children's cries. Our friendship is enabling me; somehow — outside this place poetry is supposedly fostered, as real people enjoy life in full view of the river, amid families and these delicious sounds of children — I have come back down, after many months, to the reality of poetry.

* * *

Jeff Spurgeon
Annie Bergen
Elliot Forrest
Terrance McKnight

That is the rhythm of my day, a rhythm that calms me.
I've been trying to find some basis, some solidity.
Today, I finally started to again in the tai chi
of Slow, Low and No.

Defoe in 1665 on the tai chi of slow, low and no:
"Till this week the city continued free,
there having never any died,
except that one Frenchman whom I mentioned before,
within the whole ninety-seven parishes.
Now there died four within the city,
one in Wood Street, and two in Crooked Lane."

That is the rhythm of slow. Defoe goes on:
"We had no such thing as printed newspapers in those days
to spread rumours and reports of things,
and to improve them by the invention of men,
as I have lived to see practice since.
But such things as were gathered from the letters of merchants
who corresponded abroad,

and from them was handed about by word of mouth only;
so that things did not spread instantly over the whole nation,
as they do now."

"The spread" when the market tanked and when the markets tanked
in New York in the Cubist year 2020
we knew that everyone knew what the news told us we knew.
New Yorkers are survivors of the "spread."

* * *

Igor Stravinsky
Divertimento from *The Fairy's Kiss: Danses suisses*
Houston Symphony Orchestra
Hans Graf, conductor

Sergei Rachmaninoff
Piano Concerto No. 2 in C Minor, Op. 18
Daniil Trifonov, piano
The Philadelphia Orchestra
Yannick Nézet-Séguin, conductor

* * *

I am reading "A discussion of the work of Larry Rivers"
published in *ARTnews* (Founded 1902), from March, 1961
and who do you think the author was?
Larry Rivers, of course!
He writes about growing up in the Bronx
with his Polish (or maybe Russian) born parents
his father played mazurkas, polkas and kozochkas on the violin

He writes of his parents: "I can't think of anything they did which, if I had
had the chance, I would do. No matter, if I did, I'd then be them. I praise
them for passing on to me their strength, their natural physical endurance
and animal concentration. Without it I'd be lost. So much in the making
of art is energy, energy to power the mind as it insists through a barrage of
endless interruptions..."

Yes... I praise them for passing on to me their strength
But who are they?
Today, they would seem to be Russian...
Stravinsky, Rachmaninoff, his parents, my grandparents...
Frank O'Hara looks on from across the page bemusedly
naked, hands atop his head,
except for a pair of galoshes and his name

* * *

And not to forget (how could I?) Tatyana Grosman...

* * *

And Alexander Glazunov
He'd written a *Chopiniana*
for Ballets Russes
it premiered at the Mariinsky
in St. Petersburg
and then, as *Les Sylphides*,
at Théâtre du Châtelet

the characters are the sylphs
and the poet...

* * *

Vladimir Horowitz looks out the window
lights a cigarette, adjusts the cuff of his sleeve.
He is thinking of Schubert, the Schubert of
Schwanengesang, Ständchen.
Then he gets up, walks over to the piano,
and plays it.
There is no one else in the room.

* * *

There is no one else in the room but there are a million beings in the body
more or less harmoniously dancing the dance of self.

What our predecessors once called "navel gazing"
and we called "finding ourselves"
is all the rage now! We have found ourselves!
We are prisoners of the dancing world of molecules and cells,
auditoriums for dancing, lit strings of DNA.
Get microscopes, everyone. If not in New York, telescopes.
Navel microscopes! Telescopes for stars having sex in a million windows.
If I go to prison for the crimes I haven't yet been caught for
I would like to do time in New York, in a room with a view if possible.
Money has been replaced by the abundance of play and music.
The prisoners in real prisons would kill for our freedom.
They probably have already, and know just what to do when they leave.
There is no escape from New York, but we can see the movie.
The planet is relieved to see humanity in prison: all those diggers
earth-movers soil-disturbers tree-cutters flesh-eaters animal-hunters
smoke-makers fossil-fuckers species-reducers synthesizers
of the myriad fruits of the garden to make commercial whole foods
of apples and flowers and mushrooms!
The planet rejoices in our quarantine!
Our bodies are full of dancing prisoners of the dictator Self.
In millions of quarantined rooms the tools of self-discovery
wait observation and sharing out of the windows.
Look at all the people singing together on balconies in Naples.
Likewise within us sing bodies and antibodies.
There is no cure there is no luck there is only the planetary idea
that we must slow down and join the cosmic dance.
It would be nice to have lunch at a great restaurant
but you and I are great restaurants where every sound carries far.
These are the benefits of social paralysis.
I prefer them to the adrenaline of war. It's time out.
We are making from the extraterrestrial virus of the language of Ovid
a companion, Covid, the first exiled Romanian bat.
The iPhone just lit up to say that Amazon
is not sending us anything inessential.
I hope they don't mean microscopes and telescopes.
But even if. When we eat our dearest or will be eaten by them
we'll see with the naked eye just how marvelous we are.
We are solitary cannibals now, why not know everything?

* * *

Last night I had a dream
I was walking around somewhere
There were a lot of people
Then I went over to Bernie Sanders' place
It was in the middle of a city
Probably New York, but it also had a European feel

It was a loft building
I went up in a freight elevator
Bernie was there with some other people
A large, expansive space, many rooms
Different open areas
Bernie greeted me and then went off with some people
There were various activities going on simultaneously
He was friendly but occupied, there were things to do

I went further in and was greeted by Bernie's wife, Jane
She welcomed me into a quieter area
She seemed very nurturing
I felt calm

* * *

In Prospect Park, Brooklyn, yesterday, March 20, 2020, the Spring Equinox
opened daffodils forsythia and buds listened to their orders opening when
we passed
young men and women unveiled the tattoos they hid all winter
under bulky sweaters
children budded out of their strollers racing their puppies
balls and kites in the fragrant air
joggers flinging sweat flashed by.
Our choice: six feet away or six feet under.
We rushed back home to the Land of Zoom.
Spring this year and maybe always disguises nature's order to reproduce in
endorphins.
Oh irresistible endorphin!
I am now going to listen to the Russians Vincent mentioned above.
My dreams have been boring
maybe the music will make them more interesting

I hope I never dream about Bernie singing.
In the coming world of virtual pleasures a question floats like a virus
in the air of the future:
how will one make a living in ether?

Happy 103d birthday, Vera Lynn!

* * *

CANTO
TRES

We are hunkered down
I think of Ted's poem
And I was already thinking
I needed to hunker down
Before, in early January
I made the decision
To be true to my people
As well as to my art

Now people are sheltering in place
They are receiving curbside delivery
What is happening?
The planet is sick
We knew it was happening
We kept warning each other
But only each other were listening

Now winter is over
Spring is happening
How many more springs?

* * *

We've been watching Anthony Bourdain's series *No Reservations*
It is heartening to see the imagery in places he visits
Cambodia, Haiti, Brazil, Joshua Tree
How he is able to interact, the intelligence he brings to the encounter
And the sadness at the end of every episode

* * *

This poem is turning me into Mayakovski an ignorant giant in love
with every woman individually and everyone in the Soviet Union
a country he saw as a Rubik's Cube of love
until his best friend Sergey Yesenin committed suicide
and friends and lovers started disappearing in the camps

where their poems gained weight and started swinging like barbells on the
   Kremlin

Poems! cried the apparatchiks and future oligarchs! Poems are coming for
   us!

And the poems did, becoming heavier and heavier like rockets of tungsten
   Poems!

"evil beings from outer space hungry for human innards lungs in particular"
   howled the oligarchs of the future but they were the first victims.

                                  * * *

Ozarks is a toponym
You dig?
They think it's from the French
Well, probably
But what it means?
(meaning is overrated)
But let's say it was *aux Arcs*
And further, that that was short
For *aux Arkansas*
Was "Arkansas" *really* what the French
Called what the Illinois people
Called the Quapaw?

But maybe *aux arcs* refers to
Arcs? Specifically, arcs in the
(what is now known as)
the Arkansas River
but there is also the Osage tree
its fruit is the beautiful spiked Osage orange
(looks I see now like the Corona virus)
and the wood of the Osage tree that the French
explorers called "Bois d'arc" because it was
the perfect wood for making bows.
The Native Americans taught them that
and how to make arrow heads from cert,
the stone that is a layer of the Ozarks plateau.
I found many arrow heads in dry stream beds
only some of them whole and hundreds of them mistakes.

Speaking of arcs...
Last night I was reading
A poem by John Ashbery
(I almost wrote "Josh"
Or maybe "Joshbery")
Entitled "A Mourning Forbidding
Valediction" (a coincidence
In itself, as I've been studying
Donne's "Valediction : Forbidding
Mourning" since finding
It was one of the poems Lowell
Taught in a poetry-writing workshop
At Harvard in the mid-'70s)

But in the Ashbery poem
(a long poem in seven eight-line
Stanzas, full of Donne-esque flourishes),
He uses the word "bight" :

                    "...her
Nose protruded beyond the outline of the bight
Some saw beyond, and her raincoat."

("A Mourning Forbidding Valediction" was
published in *Broadway 2: A Poets and Painters Anthology*, 1989,
edited by James Schuyler and Charles North)

Putting that journal down,
I pick up Megan Marshall's
Fantastic memoir/biography
Of Elizabeth Bishop,
A Miracle for Breakfast
And read this:

"The winter after the accident, they returned to Florida, where the island community of Key West, at the southernmost tip of the peninsula, enchanted them both. They bought a house together at 624 White Street, bankrolled by Louise, a simple two-story wooden 'eyebrow' house standing alone on its block midway between the town's two sheltered bights where fishing boats moored..."

Bringing me back, with not a lot
Of geographical hopping,
To the *arcs* of *aux arcs*
As "bight" comes from the
Old English word meaning
Bend, or bay, typically
A bend or curve in the shore
Of a sea or river
In this case, the Arkansas
where I lived seven years as a semi-hermit.

But *aux arcs* can also mean
Where the arches are
Referring to dozens of
Natural bridges in the region
Formed by erosion and
Collapsed caves.

I had a morning cave and a night cave.
The morning cave had two limestone benches
on either side of a spring that gushed from miles
of limestone below, the sweetest tasting water.
In the morning the sun burst through the mouth
of the cave, and I tried to get there in the dark
before sunrise, to meditate to the gurgle and wash
my face and drink from it. The birds outside were loud
but the cave was breathing profound silence
in its two large chambers that narrowed somewhere
only Gulliver my dachshund had explored by disappearing.
One day we looked for him all night with flashlights
calling his name. We heard him barking for a time,
then silence. We were sure then that he had fallen in
one of the many lakes that flow under the vast system
of caves under the Ozarks plateau from Arkansas to Illinois,
passing on their way the cave where Tom Sawyer kissed Becky Thatcher.

After that sleepless night next morning Gulliver returned muddy tired
    scratched and hungry.
He had found his way through the subterranean rock and came out of a hill
    somewhere.
What he had seen and fought we will never know, I wish dogs could speak
    human.

I sat with friends on the limestone cave benches. We watched the sun come up.
I called it Plato's cave, but it was the poets' cave where poets hid after Plato
   exiled them.
I know now that my cave (still there) prepared the hermitage we live in now.
"We'll bomb them back to the Stone Age," George Bush said after 9/11.
Who bombs who what bombs out we are all bombed out at the moment.

Ozarks might even be an abbreviation
For *aux arcs-en-ciel*
(toward the rainbows)
Which are a common sight there
(are they?)
triple rainbows often.

But I have another theory
(way out, but aren't all theories?)
Maybe it's from *aux arches*
Meaning "to the arks"
Meaning let's get the hell out of here before it's too late!
Or, look the enemy is here, pick up your bows!

Il faudrait peut-être nous construire une arche!
Maybe we should build ourselves an ark!

We are different and unique like all people
and when we mixed with the animals on the biblical ark
it was so they could reproduce when we reached land
so we could eat them when we ran out of food
but a new hybrid race was born on that ark
and we are that race.
The animals ate Noah and the other humans
and when they reached land took their names
and told no one the real story,
which is that we are part bat and giraffe and swan.

We share much with animals but mostly the solitude
of the deep caves and the untold stories of who we really are.
We have probably forgotten them but they are still there
available only to solitude and quarantine.
The dreams of my patients, a therapist friend tells me,
are remarkable these days, so different than those they told Before.

Geologic

SILENCE FOR STEVE DALACHINSKY WHO SAW IT COMING
AND LEFT ON STAGE LIKE THE PERFORMER HE WAS
SILENCE FOR ALL THE PEOPLE WE KNEW WELL OR SLIGHTLY
STILL FLOATING IN THE NEW YORK MARCH AIR
THE AIR OF THE HOLY DAYS OF REBIRTH

I will write a verse for every siren, said Ovid
caught in the classical emergency of his endless exile
my fate is to move from place to place until I return home
but no one has yet told me where that is
in the background of the blaring sirens outside a symphony
from the air raids of the last century and the emergencies of this one

I walk to the Flushing Meadows of Corona Park the ash heap
that F. Scott Fitzgerald disliked and Robert Moses
turned into the site of two World's Fairs.
Every day I walk three times around the Unisphere
the point zero of mid-century American optimism.
I see the Corona Virus too in rusting steel threatening the Unisphere.
This is the rough cement and steel map of Now.

Now is the moment of care it is Lynnea and all others struggling to care for
    those suffering those
dying at the hands of this reprehensible disease which is the disease of our
    civilization

We caused this make no mistake the politicians but we too were complicit
    we are all guilty and
all deserve credit for all creations and warmth expressed by the genome

I had to find a place open to buy a coffee
And found a place I've often been to
All the others, even ones I went to last week, are now closed
They've been trying curbside delivery and takeout
We've all been trying to support them in this small way,
And other ways, if possible

Now, it seems, they can no longer take the pain
So breathe in the pain
Breathe out some help, some happiness, some humor

The place I did get coffee
Had to let all its employees go
All applying for unemployment
The owner has been working 100 hours a week
22 days straight

Hold your head down
Crouch
Wait for the blast
Try to keep clean

We don't understand any of this

Ted wrote a poem in which he
Used the phrase "hunker down"
I've always thought of it
Always imagined him doing it
And what it meant
Now everyone in their own way does

* * *

I read A.C.'s poems in *Big Sky* 2 (1972), Box 272, Bolinas, CA, Bill Berkson, Editor

Works by: Ginsberg, Gallup, di Prima, Creeley, Brainard, Schuyler, Mathews, Borregaard, Obenzinger, Whalen, Berrigan, Codrescu, Elmslie, MacAdams, Padgett, Giorno, Waldman, Clark, Coolidge, Brownstein, Fagin, Veitch, Notley, Kyger, Warsh, et al

Cover: Alex Katz portrait of Edwin Denby smiling with "BIG SKY" in rough hand lettering

Berrigan's poem : "Upon the river, point me out my course"

Andrei's : "watching Ted shoot up / is both sad and mythical."

put on Mozart *Symphony in D Major* written in Rome when he was 14

Mendelsohn's *Sixth String Symphony* written when he was 12-14

He sparked Bach revival with performance of *St. Matthew Passion*

* * *

We knew everything the young know everything they are fearless
we poets have no choice even as death spreads her wings and translates
us into the matter of a universe that redistributes what is useful
we keep the memories that in their turn join other memories
of so many carnivals – *carne vale* – that the cross of ashes cannot obliterate
even if you made it at the bar direct from the ashtray on Mardi Gras night
I am grateful to the fighters and the fighting poets Whitman Louis Aragon
Paul Eluard Elsa Triolet Anna Akhmatova Mayakovski Pasternak
Sandburg Emma Lazarus Tristan Tzara Mina Loy all the brave frontline
word slingers who said it plain and clear as the disasters of their time unfolded
around them mowing down the wordless and the scared shitless

Yup it's our turn

We started out not speaking the name of the plague

or the names of the greedy pig viruses that beguile us on vampyr TV
but our masks are ready and caution to the wind poets
What's to be Done? as Lenin and Chernishevski said
the question Dada and the 20th century fresh then had to answer and
the answer that knocked the old world down
and made the world we live in now

a window on rows of commie cement towers
the inmates out to ring cowbells and holler
in New York howls of appreciation
they say got the frontline doctors and nurses
but a howl of rage at the orange stain on TV screens
its puss infects the republic

* * *

To hunker down
To remember Ted Berrigan and all the others who have gone before and
    are gone
To remember Memorial Day
To remember Joe Brainard

To think of a sound ricocheting off a guitar string, then slicing downward
    into a person's gullet,
From which another sound, voice, is uttered
Guttered, Simile-ed, Cried, Outgrown, Unnerved
Backed into a grove
In which a poet sits underneath a tree, singing quietly in the cold

* * *

The Officers of the Academy note with sorrow the death of the artist Wolf
Kahn, of New York, on Sunday, March Fifteenth, Two Thousand Twenty,
at the age of ninety-two

The Officers of the Academy note with sorrow the death of the composer
Charles Wuorinen, of New York, on Wednesday, March Eleventh, Two
Thousand Twenty, at the age of eighty-one

"I said why not invite other artists to join us and give works, and then we'll be able to help others. That's how it started." — Jasper Johns

The Merce Cunningham Award
The Roy Lichtenstein Award
The Robert Rauschenberg Award
The Dorothea Tanning Award
The C.D. Wright Award for Poetry
The Helen Frankenthaler Award for Painting
The Cy Twombly Award for Poetry
The John Cage Award
The Ellsworth Kelly Award

* * *

"I used to lock up my writings along with my cigarettes in a file cabinet so my mother couldn't see them. I considered poetry a matter of profound embarrassment because not only was it considered cheesy but because I could derive from this supposedly cheesy thing the best kind of feeling from reading and making it, the kind that gave me chills. And I wanted to impart that feeling to others."
—Julian Talamantez Brolaski

* * *

Easter Oratorio, BWV 249, Johann Sebastian Bach
Amsterdam Baroque Choir

* * *

Sarabande and Rigaudon, Op. 93, Camille Saint-Saëns
Lille National Orchestra

* * *

A strange, very straightforward design of a hair dryer
That also looks like some kind of weapon
Or industrial installation

Looks like tires but they're actually brushes, brush side up
Facing you with little squiggles announcing or supporting them
And, further back, a numeration system physically dug into
The surface, perhaps plaster, perhaps clay, from 0 to 12

Two sophisticated-looking gentlemen look down at a large drawing
Spread on the floor, a series of distorted figures, brusquely drawn
With other, similar drawings, some more filled in with color, spread
Around them on the floor, and still others, more like drawn paintings,
With even more color added, stacked up against the wall behind them

* * *

I dreamt that I was sleeping and in my dream
I said let's dream some more and I did.
Outside the wind that was here after demolishing 100 houses in Nashville
and wrecking the South with tornadoes raged between the brick towers
of Queens knocking down trees and I saw the spirally thing at the top
of the high school Joey Ramone went to (Joey Ramone Alley now)
sway like the future that used to be rockets and spirals and the cosmos in 1966
at the "peak of American optimism" now more modestly aiming to "flatten
     the curve."
Nothing points upward anymore, though young men must be restless in their
     caves
filled with the not-so-fun family including the homeless and the orphans
brought in by the authorities that distributed them to everyone with a roof.
I know, not yet, but you just wait. My favorite movie is *Ninotchka*,
and I saw *The Death of Stalin*, and something like nostalgia almost blew by.

This is Monday, April 13, 2020, in the Year of the Plague.
Locusts have covered Africa.
In the introduction to the Apocalypse, the numbers and specific features of
     the plagues
were catalogued, but the real thing by John of Patmos was a lot like this.
Plagues resemble each other, they see us as animals do. A wild cat looks at
     humans:
hunkered in their cubicles, eyes burned by screen light.
They "feel" things and a preacher on TV says "feelings are God."
What nonsense. We have all read *Madame Bovary* by Dr. Gustave Flaubert,

who said, "Every notary carries within him the remains of a poet!"
Now if only the Plague would be as kind to us as our cats.
And my notary charges me fees for legal papers while the poet within cowers.
I want those grants named after painters now!

* * *

The Rub' al Khali, the Empty Quarter of the Arabian Peninsula

Only the greatest desert specialists can survive here

This is one of their last refuges

This oldest of deserts

* * *

"Only the dead have seen the end of war" — Plato

* * *

I've always thought I prefer
Not to completely decipher the lyrics of songs I love
As my friend Paul once said, apropos Led Zeppelin,
"I know all these songs by heart, even the ones
I can't understand completely"

Now, listening to the Stones sing "Tumbling Dice,"
I think, "I could look these lyrics up now" and finally
Know for sure what they say
But I don't, I prefer to relax in my knowing
Which is the knowing of listening
To what I myself hear
Which is what I have always heard there

* * *

The Delaware was named for Thomas West,
3rd Baron De La Warr, who waged a punitive war
Against the Powhatan, who had killed the Virginia Colony's
First president, John Ratcliffe

The Jamestown settlers wanted to pack it in,
Head back to England, where, at least, the brutality
Was one they were culturally accustomed to
But West's counterattack convinced them to remain

Delaware was originally part of William Penn's
Pennsylvania Colony, the Duke of York granted
Penn access to the sea via the Delaware Bay
These lower counties remained until Delaware
Separated from Pennsylvania on June 15, 1776

* * *

Now, on a Sunday in Pennsylvania, I am listening to
Rosmonda d'Inghilterra, an opera in two acts by
Gaetano Donizetti that had its premiere at Teatro
Della Pergola in Florence in 1834
It was largely forgotten until rediscovered by
Patric Schmid in 1975

It's not so much the story right now but rather
The beautifully composed melodies and phrasing
Of the orchestral accompaniment that is
Providing nourishment on this still-cold spring day
A piccolo solo just now breaks through

Earlier, I was listening to Caetano Veloso
Interviewing a young Brazilian Marxist

on "portrait of a young brazilian marxist"
it was noted that soccer and bikinis in copacabana
are ideological like everything else except carmen miranda
whose museum in Rio we were unable to visit
because all the directions to it were wrong
a lot like the roads leading from marx to lenin stalin
and all the rest of the stuffed suits seated on the dais
at may 1st parades watching missiles tanks and pioneers
no bikinis or samba in those processions
(except for the ones in Fidel's Cuba)

"In the Red Army Club at the Kremlin," (1927)
"a map of Europe hangs on the wall. Beside it
a crank is turned: it shows all the places Lenin passed
in the course of his life... little electric lights flash...
Simbirsk, Kazan, Petersburg, Geneva, Cracow, Zürich,
Moscow, up to the place of his death, Gorki.
Lenin's life resembles a campaign of colonial conquest.
Citizens study Germany on a map of Poland, France,
or even Denmark; but on a map of Russia they see
Europe as a little frayed, nervous territory far out to the west."
(Walter Benjamin, *Reflections*, 1929)

In the mausoleum Lenin's head is embalmed with newspapers.
Today many other platforms were added inside Lenin's head.
Lenin's head now has Google, Zoom, FaceTime and Pandemic Hourly.
You only need to dial Lenin's head and you can interview Marx, Benjamin,
Adorno, and any Brazilian Marxist.

Of course Lenin's head info is censored and his password is unlisted.
Only a select few know it: it is ERROR. Dial ERROR. Stay away
at least six feet from your screen because a blast of Russian winter
blows and can freeze you like a Siberian mammoth in historic ice.

Lenin's head is also known as The Oracle of the Kremlin.
You can ask, for example, how long we are going to be locked up.
He usually says, "Ask Stalin. Just getting to Siberia takes a long time."
But sometimes he says, "If you have a gun, shoot the enemy. Then
you won't be locked up at all, you will be shot immediately."
Marxism is not a choice if you don't like answers and have too many
questions. In New York in 2020 there are as many Marxists as Covid dead.

CANTO CUATRO

"Those little yellow flowers there — they think they have a place in the world!"

—Ada, 3/28/20

A pause in the empty town,
Green bridge in offing, car
Whooshes, ascends to it,
Bright light gives coherence, wind
Blows general store sign back and forth,
A few tiny clouds seem embarrassed
In the great blue apocalypse

(Stockton, NJ, 4/22/20, Earth Day)

* * *

The days of my quarantine begin to order themselves:
I recall last night's dream: a car full of my dead relatives
arrives to make room for me to go to a great family picnic.
My young cousin still living in Alba Iulia,
an ancient town in Transylvania,
informs me that the bandit Matta has been captured.
He had killed my grandfather in 1938 but now in 2020
my grandfather is alive and tells jokes. I am it seems my father.

I must attend the picnic in Bucharest 300 km away
without delay, so I ask if she's a robot and she laughs.

The recording of this scene is on my iPhone for a half hour.
I call it "The iPad cemetery" and I must urgently tell Tim Cook
or Bill Gates how it works before someone who reads this poem
steals it. I decide not to go the family picnic but to California,
where my friend Lewis MacAdams lives and knows everybody.

I write the above in my iPhone Notes.
During the transatlantic flight on Virgin Air
I read *Waves Passing in the Night* by Ren Weschler,
a book about the great music of the spheres
as discovered by the great sound designer Walter Murch.
Walter lives in Bolinas where Lewis MacAdams
and his wife Phoebe also live long before this dream.

In my dream Lewis is still the Water Commissioner
of Bolinas, the only elected job in the small town,
and also the editor of *Wet: a Magazine of Gourmet Bathing*,
where I call him often just to hear the receptionist say dreamily, "Weeeat."
Lewis conceived the 100-year-plan to resurface the Los Angeles River,
a plan that bore fruit in his lifetime.
Lewis was a poet, a gentleman, a Texan,
father of children, serious about serious things, and merry
about funny things.
He wasn't home when my plane landed.

Lewis died last night, the night of Earth Day, April 21, 2020, in Los Angeles.
May those angels carry you to the Big Sky River, friend, Water God.

* * *

I love the way he flows through the strings
Like a breeze blowing through leaves
Near a river at the end of day
It's gotten a little colder
The summer is cold suddenly

Then there's a dance

(Sibelius's treatment of *The Tempest*)

* * *

"Paracelsus spoke for such length of time
his listeners often died of old age." – Aleister Crowley

"I start the day counting my wealth, feeding the animals, satisfying my
hungers, splitting wood and singing." – Alexander von Humboldt

"Find caveats, look for them, they will absolve you from finishing wrongly
the speech of others." – Confucius

The reason you must not finish anyone's sentence
is that you never know how they will finish that sentence
they will never finish it the way you do

you think you know how they will finish it but you don't
you are a prisoner of time in quarantine like everyone else
who finishes another's sentence for one's convenience
but the speaker of it might finish it radically, by suicide
not words, for example, and how can you finish such
a sentence, a death sentence you are sharing but not in
or never in words. This caveat is a note to self.
Pin it on the refrigerator, that time-capsule squatting
like a god at the center of your life, as every sentence
has a center of gravity also in the pause between words
where you are tempted to enter as in an open door
to finish it for them. It is the forbidden door in the fairy tale.
Should I listen to our world from the future I hear
mostly broken sentences spoken by many voices
a habit of speech that scrambles knowledge and advances
wisdom, the wisdom of sparing one the end. The end
of the sentence, death. It is a kindness to take on another's
sentence and finish it. A kindness that is not benign,
a kindness that fears the truth, the end, the unfolding
of thought and its unpredictable dying in its last words.
All sentences are pregnant.

* * *

And their babies are Poetry, Drama, and a Log of Days.
Their abortions are Spell Check and Auto Correct.
I practice three forms of poetry now in the Days of the Plague.
A Dream Journal on my iPhone (approx 30 minutes)
Tai Chi (20 minutes)
A poem based on reading poetry or philosophy.
Writing this in English in The Epic of Care collaboration.
Writing in Romanian in the poetry collaboration with Carmen Firan
now called "Tabla Mendeleev" (the "Mendeleev Table of Elements")
where each of us is an element: today Carmen is Pt (Platinum)
and I am Au (Gold). Carmen and I also wrote "Alfabetul." ("The Alphabet").
Each one of us was a letter — there are two extra letters in Romanian:
"Tz" (Carmen) and "She" (me).

* * *

When Marta Argerich plays Mozart's 20th *Piano Concerto*, as conducted by Claudio Abbado, it's not about the speed but rather the density of experience, her left leaning into, prodding, but never overturning her right, her runs balanced, mellifluous. It's all about the pushing and ultimate balance.

* * *

Leon Fleisher playing *Piano Concerto 23* of Mozart with the Stuttgart Chamber Orchestra

He gently banishes the stormclouds

It's always the adagio that gets you

That's the one

Thank god for the adagio

* * *

There's a photo of Humbert Lucarelli, cradling his oboe in the nook of his left arm, resting his left elbow on a light-wood (perhaps walnut) pianoforte, his right hand tucked in his pocket.

He played the *Idillio-Concertino* of Hermano Wolf-Ferrari.

Based in Chicago, Humbert is also known in the New York area. He's in his eighties now.

In the photo, he's wearing a black tux and bow tie, leaning in toward the photographer. We can see some vegetation through the open windows, sheet music on the piano's stand, and we wonder, deeply, what is outside those windows.

* * *

We hermits log our hours in ways as different (or as similar) as music and memory

as different as listening and remembering, as fine as practice of a skill and theory.
We men from different origins, places, and of different age, bring our
   common beings
into the space of this poem like actors auditioning on a stage
as vast as the world that unfolds day by day and night by night in history.
Make no mistake, reader, this play is history, and history will not rest
until the sun sets in the East and rises in the West — then we will lie down
   in earth's
immense embrace like the children we are and will sink deep
in a dreamless sleep. I see us, Vincent and I, like Don Quixote and Sancho Panza,
taking turns at being one or the other, unless you think otherwise, fighting
   the windmills
from Queens, Vermont, Maine, Brooklyn, Europe and Korea,
our verses like lances always ready to defend the honor of our beloved Dulcinea.

* * *

I see it exactly the same way, changing roles,
Shape-shifting, that's the way it's going to be
From now on

But she's educated, doesn't give a damn,
She's very complicated...
Looks so simple in her way,
Does the same things every day,
But she's dedicated to having her own way,
She's very complicated...

It might be until the sun sets on the West,
Sets on the East...

But somehow, this music, the stuff
We always listened to, still is the nourishing
Food that keeps us going in these times
People keep calling strange
How long can something remain strange?

An electric guitar chunking out a rhythm
A tom riff huddles in the murk

We are hiding out in different spots

* * *

A bird singing this morning in two pitches, an A flat and a B, in three notes, one on the A flat and two on the B just above, reminded me of what I need to be: gentle.

* * *

The dolphins are such geniuses.
Against all odds, they convince
the False Killer Whales pursuing
them to be their friends. At the
ultimate moment of the kill, they
turn
and face them
and seem
to speak or sing to them. Then
they sing too, and the two species
have a giant party, going off
in search of fish to eat.

* * *

A kind of giant wrasse called the Kobudai, also known as the Asian
    sheepshead wrasse
Made its spectacular media debut near Sado Island in Japan in 2017
It is a striking-looking animal, who is hermaphroditic and changes sex
    during its lifetime
Japanese diver Hiroyuki Arakawa has known a specific Kobudai for 30 years
He calls it to his underwater Shinto shrine by ringing a bell
Then, I imagine, they are happy to see each other and hang out for a while

* * *

It's May Day! Yes!
We made it to May
And can celebrate
The workers, ones
Who really get shit
Done, who know

The real clock, sock
Hours into machines,
Not sweating in suits,
But honest shirts and
Pants — but the others,
Who want to rise,
Believe in the ladder,
Them we must watch,
Ones who listen to falsehoods,
Drawn to denigration,
Exaggeration,
We all are at times,
But need unions,
Need to hunker down
In meetings, unapologetic,
Unapoplectic, able
To sit down today,
Even after many beers,
To figure a way out.

* * *

Every day sea becomes land
And land becomes sea

* * *

When he was 20 years old and came to New York
David was looking at paintings at MoMA
and his Italian friend said, "In New York there is no time."
Yes, you can say then that time had been suspended
but it was still metaphorical. The city never slept
for anyone who wanted to do something at night. I was
working the night shift too until 1970 when I went to San Francisco
and found mornings fresher for having slept the night.
Art is what artists do with the night. In the years
of amphetamines and sex, night was its playground in New York.
In San Francisco the ocean and the fog took art to nature
which prefers mornings for opening its buds and breathing.
In Italy where I lived next there was little distinction between day and night.

I preferred night in Rome and mornings in Naples to hide from tourists.
An artist, I reasoned, somehow was not a tourist. An artist worked.
The philistine tourists in Rome saw in the morning the art I made at night.
The lazy tourists in Naples saw art beginning in the afternoon.
From 1965 until 1983 everyone had a hangover and art was palliative.
The cure for artists was art. And the zoo. When I lived in Baltimore
I often spent the night drinking in the company of Anselm Hollo
and in the morning we went to the zoo. The animals there healed us.
They looked on us with compassion and without judgement.
Compassionate zebra! Kind furry medium-sized beings! Darling elephants!
For artists every city kept a different time, optimal to their flowering.

Now time is a jello cube we are all embedded in everywhere on the planet.
The jello wobbles in a nauseating succession of hours
days months years that do not inspire anything except decay.
I'm in New York where everything was once urgent but now it's not.
The vigor of morning is lacking and so is the fever of the night.
The rats who have been here forever own the night and the day,
At night behind lit windows the masses make neither art nor love.
They eat carbohydrates or exercise muscles nobody appreciates.
Art does not like the night here or the day. How selfless we were in time!
What we made was not about us, it was about the human world.
Next year the humans will starve for meat but also for free concerts in the park.
When they come out like frenzied rats only music will hydrate
The dryness we suffered in quarantine. The only thing dry will be
Police nightsticks cracking our heads for being so happy as to break the law.
Even the whoosh of bullets on through the flesh of our bodies will be
     sweet music
When they return time, day and night, to us. I will make art when I see
     you again.
There won't be any revolution but a lot of real estate for me to make my hours.

* * *

Let's make art when we get out of here
We're making art but I know what you mean
The art of walking freely, of randomly meeting
People one does or doesn't know
The vigor and the fever are out there
We will find them

It's Monday and Breakfast for Bach is happening
The Collegium Musicale does
Herr, wie du willt, so schicks mit mir, BWV 73
Cantata by Johann Sebastian Bach
Composed in 1724, when Bach was 39
First performed in Leipzig on the 23rd of January of that year

He'd arrived there the year previous
And started writing cantatas for the city's churches
For this particular Sunday, the required texts were
From *Epistle to the Romans* — Romans 12:17-21 —

17 Be not wise in your own conceit. Recompense to no man evil for evil. Provide things honest in the sight of all men.

18 If it be possible, as much as lieth in you, live peaceably with all men.

19 Dearly beloved, avenge not yourselves, but rather give place unto wrath: for it is written, Vengeance is mine; I will repay, saith the Lord.

20 Therefore if thine enemy hunger, feed him; if he thirst, give him drink: for in so doing thou shalt heap coals of fire on his head.

21 Be not overcome of evil, but overcome evil with good.

And from *Matthew 8:1-13* —

Which is about healing a leper
The unknown poet takes the words of the leper
"Lord, if thou wilt, thou canst make me clean"
And makes trust the key factor
In facing death

But that could be equally true
In facing life

1 When he was come down from the mountain, great multitudes followed him.

2 And, behold, there came a leper and worshipped him, saying, Lord, if thou wilt, thou canst make me clean.

3   And Jesus put forth his hand, and touched him, saying, I will; be thou clean. And immediately his leprosy was cleansed.

4   And Jesus saith unto him, See thou tell no man; but go thy way, shew thyself to the priest, and offer the gift that Moses commanded, for a testimony unto them.

5   And when Jesus was entered into Capernaum, there came unto him a centurion, beseeching him,

6   And saying, Lord, my servant lieth at home sick of the palsy, grievously tormented.

7   And Jesus saith unto him, I will come and heal him.

8   The centurion answered and said, Lord, I am not worthy that thou shouldest come under my roof: but speak the word only, and my servant shall be healed.

9   For I am a man under authority, having soldiers under me: and I say to this man, Go, and he goeth; and to another, Come, and he cometh; and to my servant, Do this, and he doeth it.

10 When Jesus heard it, he marveled, and said to them that followed, Verily I say unto you, I have not found so great faith, no, not in Israel.

11 And I say unto you, That many shall come from the east and west, and shall sit down with Abraham, and Isaac, and Jacob, in the kingdom of heaven.

12 But the children of the kingdom shall be cast out into outer darkness: there shall be weeping and gnashing of teeth.

13 And Jesus said unto the centurion, Go thy way; and as thou hast believed, so be it done unto thee. And his servant was healed in the selfsame hour.

JSB collaged text, taking from the Good Book
And also from Kaspar Bienemann's chorale, *Jeremiah 17:9* and Ludwig
    Helmbold's hymn
"Von Gott will ich nicht lassen"

"Ludwig Helmbold was one of the principal poets of his day, and published a number of Latin odes and elegies, for which the Emperor Maximilian, at the Diet of Augsburg, awarded him the honours and emoluments of poet-laureate. Of his German writings the odes are said to be very poor, but he was a fertile song-writer both for the school and home, after the manner of Nikolaus Herman, and for the Church. One of his hymns is to be found in all German hymn-books, and has rooted itself among the people. It was written in 1563, when a terrible pestilence attacked Erfurt, and in the course of a year destroyed 4,000 of its inhabitants, so that the university had to be broken up for some months. Helmbold gave this hymn to the wife of one of his friends, as she was starting on a hasty flight from the city; and in most of the old hymn-books it is headed 'The True Christian's Vade-Mecum'." [bach-cantatas.com]

* * *

Money has a strange knowledge

* * *

Radio-Activity, released in 1975,
Was their first fully electronic album
Florian's role in the band
Layers on top
Atmospheres
Sound design
The album is like...
50% making references to the radio
And 50% references to radioactivity
And blurring the line between the two

The creations of Kraftwerk
And the work of Florian Schneider especially
He passed on April 21, 2020,
14 days after his 73rd birthday
And here is *Radio-Activity*
Let's stay tuned and see
What happens next

* * *

When money talks, no one listens.
What did money say when the plague came?
You have enough of me to run away?
But where will you go when everyone is there?

I can help you run away from your own corpse
but for a limited time only and then I can buy you a grave
In Père Lachaise with words by poets on the black stone.
Money said peevishly: tomorrow will not make breakfast.
I will disappear and you must steal your eggs.
Money also said I will soon be a rarity like edelweiss.
You'll see me only if you climb this mountain and when, bathed in sweat,
you smell fragrant to me I'll shower you with gold flakes like a nymph.
If you don't know, nymphs give off a scent of sweet olive and lust.
Also, youth is the only currency, and I, money, am old.
I am bored, said money to the solitary vault where it did time
just for the crime of symbolism. If symbolism is a crime
then caviar is my revenge. Ah, money sighs, but these days
I can't even go to Paris for my yearly visit to Apollinaire.
What good am I if I can't have cassis in Cape Ferrat?
I used to have a hell of a time when I was more than a symbol.
I could rouse the rabble on TV and on the street.
I could hold myself in front of hungry mobs like meat.
I could give myself to anyone and make them do the things they wanted.
Alas. For myself these days I can think of nothing I want, and worse,
Neither can my master, who claims me as his fortune.
I have become but paper. I'd rather be a cow feeding my calves.
Symbolically I am a cow and calf, but I am sick of symbols.
Giving myself away is my only pleasure because it pleases
those who have me but I'm like a monk or a cold woman:
the pleasure is all theirs and I feel only regret and impotence.
My self-worth resides non-symbolically only in human hubris.
When distinctions disappear, I am like everything else, a movie.

That was *that* money speaking. Now listening to the guests
on Andrew Revkin's *Twitter Live* I hear myself called "complex system,"
"sustainability," "people," planet," or "people planet" (hail Hashem),
"individual," "citizen," "generational," "ecosystem," "factor," "growth,"
"globalized," "Covid," "revelation," "struggle," "security."
My mom never called me those nicknames, I feel like a ghost.
The poor, Jesus said, will always miss me.
The virus found a fragile host. I am its deep and endless maze.
I have to put on my mask and gloves now to visit myself.

* * *

Budding in hard times
Edge and Roof
Everywhere I've walked in New York this spring
I've confronted cheeriness
Daffodils
Continuous as the stars that shine
Seemingly a description of a moment
For what other have we?
Out-did the sparkling waves
For earlier poets, carried
Symbolic weight
The myths, Easter and springtime
Poems on vanity, brevity,
Death and resurrection

An insistence on a natural style

Nothing can bring back the hour
Of splendor in the grass, of glory in the flower

Or

The world is too much with us; late and soon,
Getting and spending, we lay waste our powers

But what has the sight done for him?

For oft, when on my couch I lie
In vacant or in pensive mood,
They flash upon that inward eye
Which is the bliss of solitude

Or for me?

CANTO CINCO

poets hands in pocket
such light tools
figure on the street
doing to time
what time does to us all
saying "screw it"
there isn't any
now time has another texture
like this poem it couldn't have
happened any other time
and still eternal are our tools

We come to a place this place
Medusa still there 30 seconds.
Enough to petrify the onlooker.
I come to a place of irritated calm.
I am waiting for something to explode
or someone inside me, a carnivorous flower,
a floral grenade, some violent and interesting thing.
Ropes outside the balcony, workers overhead.
I hear an airplane. On cue Carmen calls:
"Listen, there is an airplane, a hopeful thing."

This place I've come to, a swamp, static
but without reptilian charm or sulfur,
cranes or frogs or Cajuns shrimping.
Has New York become Minneapolis in 1956?
This is the place now where I feel out of place.
My wit is gone, my money is about to,
the telephone no longer signifies hope.
A still island in a tired country under self-arrest.
I can't think of a place to go, there is no place.
Where can you run when there is no place to run to?
I wish Baudelaire would drop by to dissect this ennui.

* * *

He was here, Charles, just a few minutes ago
He dropped by to say he was feeling energized
By all this: suddenly, he's not the odd man out —
When everyone is drifting toward oblivion,
The man of evil flowers is suddenly central:
The man of wandering, of the painter of
Modern life, of clothing, of albatrosses

* * *

Fear not, I am with you
Hilliard Ensemble singing Bach motet

Listening to poetry in Zoom conversation
While checking emails and writing poetry
Alternating between the Spanish original
And the English translation
Translation is something we have both
Had occasion for, a necessary passage

* * *

William, Robert, and Robert project themselves from their covers
Wordsworth, Graves, and Lowell
Painting, photo, photo
Looking sideways down, looking straight down, looking askance

Elderly, young, middle aged
While Philip waits in the hall
Standing on a boardwalk in jumper and light-colored tie

* * *

Today was the day Mozart died
It is very green outside
Most of the trees have flowered already
The peonies are out

* * *

Yesterday was my mother's birthday
We had a nice day together
She was happy
What does it mean to live so many years
On this earth?
What can possibly be the same,
Carry over from worlds one came from,
Worlds one wrought, or tried to?

Can there be continuity, as a friend sagely
Suggested was key, the one thing
To hold on to near the end, that someone,
Not something, might continue?
Someone close to one,
Who might share a world
And sharing, bring
That world better alignment?

* * *

One can only keep
Writing poetry,
That stream is continuous,
From first humans to last,
From stroking and tapping
To dispersed extremity

In the *OED*, I find, under *tenuous*:

1. Thin or slender in form; of small transverse measure or calibre; slim.

2. Thin in physical consistency; sparse; rare, rarified, subtile; unsubstantial.

3. *figurative*. Slender, of slight importance or significance; meagre, weak; flimsy, vague, unsubstantial.

It first appeared in English in 1597, in work on surgery, in which the
     author wrote,
"When the vaines are repleat with a tenous blood."
In 1892, the journal *Leisure Hour*, in its August number, published the sentence,
"A very tenuous medium called the ether exists everywhere."
And in 1909, this sentence appeared in the *English Review*:
"Your dress brushed the shrubs: it was grey and tenuous."

We have arrived at *A Nest of Ninnies*

And the way the baby groundhog
Tries its way out of its lair onto bright grass
Reminds us how tenuous everything is
We are all always hanging by a thread

There are ropes in front of my window
One for hanging and one for escaping
I will take the rope less traveled I think
when two men with hardhats appear out of the fog in a basket
with tools in their leather belts.
The basket is swaying like a small boat, it's a windy day.
I expect they will rise above my balcony to the one above
where they've been scraping and banging to fix or build something
an orgone box a pigeon coop or a greenhouse.
I smell pot wafting from up there sometimes
I hear mumbles and half sentences that sound angry
as if the men up there would like to fight someone who isn't there.
I sometimes think it's me because I am alone.
One night I'll climb up there on the rope less traveled
and tell them what I failed to say and that I masterfully
wrought in response, or they might come down from above and do to me

what I am planning for them. Together we will sound out one hell
of a fighting sentence that would end this ridiculous situation
once and for all. Now it is morning and the hard hats are rising back.

* * *

Hard hats and soldiers
Rubber bullets shot into faces
Pepper spray
The president calling for White Supremacist fascist militias
To attack peaceful protesters

What is the function of peaceful assembly?
Freedom of speech we are clued into
But peaceful assembly
We don't think about that one all the time
Peaceful protest
Is the confluence of peaceful assembly
And freedom of speech
We are still guaranteed that

And strangely, two men
We might not think of
As protectors of our rights
Are talking about them

Keeping in mind they did walk
From the White House
To St. John's Episcopal Church
The day police and National Guard
Used tear gas, smoke canisters
Pepper-spray projectiles, flash grenades,
Riot shields, batons, and brute force
To clear out peaceful protestors

«Congress shall make no law respecting an establishment of religion, or
prohibiting the free exercise thereof; or abridging the freedom of speech,
or of the press; or the right of the people peaceably to assemble, and to
petition the Government for a redress of grievances.»

We embarked on this epic focusing on the care
Needed at all times, especially this one

As coronavirus raged, and those we love
Became enmeshed, an ocean of jobs lost,
We started to name names and make it personal

Then George Floyd happened
And everything changed, again

We saw people enraged,
In beautiful communal work,
Fighting for animal survival
In streets and other public places

We also saw the bitter fruit
Of this particularly deranged leader, his whistle calls
To White Supremacist and other outlaw factions
A sickness deep in our national soul
That cannot be easily cured
It will take a deep and painful
Operation on the body politic
Ongoing therapy for the nation mind
Even those may not be enough

* * *

Today is my birthday
6/4/20

* * *

Happy birthday, my collaborator
In the criminal enterprise we concocted.
Many happy returns my colleague in the old
art of verse serving no purpose now
or at least serving less purpose than it did in "normal" times

though I am not sure what times those were
and who was asleep on the job
I suspect that this wonderful revolution
that has people rather die of Covid
than stay inside without making a gesture
is good for propaganda but not poetry

* * *

June 8. Tonglen. I am breathing in instability
And trying to breathe out stability.
Breathing in doubt and trying
To breathe out certainty. Not
A permanent certainty; that does not
Exist. But Frank O'Hara's
"Marvelous joy of being sure."
Rudy's few minutes of real happiness.
Those things do exist, even
In the picture of egolessness.

Is there an ego in seeing somebody in a crowd
who takes your breath away?
And knows it?
That wave can carry matter through time and space,
an instrument finer than whatever any lab might make.

Are you present when a small whirl of pedestrian weirdness
Involving the street and people unfolds in perfect
Filmic wonder on 12th and Broadway when the French girls
ask you in perfect innocence if they should return to Paris
or stay in New York
if they can find a place to stay?
The apartment of your heart opens with a 360 view.

Yesterday a crowd looted Strand Bookstore a celebration
Of reading if you think, knowing well
That it was nothing of the sort only the sound
Of breaking glass that crowds love most of all?
Strand's response was to donate a goodly sum
To Black Lives Matter

but that's something I just read in the paper and it means little
To me personally. I would rather look at a girl opening a book
For longer than ten seconds

* * *

Listening to a double oboe concerto
By Conrad Hurlebusch, many of whose
Works have been lost, I wonder
How many of our works may someday be lost?
What will remain is the effort, the expense,
And the attempt to reach another human being,
The awareness of the fragility of ecosystems
And the fierce spirit of living things

[6/8/20]

The fierce spirit of all living things
Living in communal strangeness is the poet key.
In Richard Wilbur's translation of Apollinaire's "Pont Mirabeau"
Lies the only thing that lives:
"How slow life seems to me
How violent the hope of love can be"
As in Ted Berrigan's Rimbaud you find:
"And I have seen what other men
Have only thought they've seen."
Those two are a sublime pair of beasts.
New York, get yourself together and let the poets out!

* * *

Time some time gets too circular! July 11-18 2020. Year of the Plague

"Hello Andrei, we met in the Lower East Side in 1967.
I was married to a Palestinian man at the time.
Before we could move into your place on Ave. C,
we bought all the furnishings in the apartment.
I have since written a book about my experience
of being captured by the Israelis while hiding
with Faisal and his family in Ramallah.

Published in 2017, *Unexpected Bride in the Promised Land: Journeys in Palestine and Israel*

It is a historical memoir that is unfortunately still relevant.

We were all so young then and meet virtually decades later.

I look forward to reading one of your books. Iris Keltz (then Iris Khatib)"

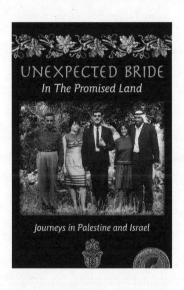

"Oh, my God! What an amazing blast from the past!

I have thought often of the scene — I may have written a version of it

somewhere — of you and Faisal coming to see the apartment —

Faisal handed me what we then called "key money," $500, I think,

from his shoe. That $500 got us to San Francisco to start a new life —

Alice was pregnant with my first, Lucian. We stayed with friends...

I told everyone that an Arab prince and his wife came to save us

from NY, a miserable place back then... A life passed — 53 years! —

I wrote books, had children, married, remarried, etc.

Three years ago I came back to New York. You don't by any chance

know of a 2 bedroom apt for rent? That would make the perfect circle.

Phenomenal. I'll also read your book, of course. Where are you living

now?"

"Great to hear from you yesterday. I see that 53 years ago we shared a
    moment in time

that changed both of our lives. The apartment on Avenue C was our first
    home together.

We did not stay there too long, found a great 1BR on Ave. A overlooking Tompkins Square. Lots of windows and light. We could see a most amazing world pass by from our living room.

I am now living in Taos NM. Faisal lives in Buffalo NY. Although we are divorced we remain good friends and allies. Unfortunately, the events described in this book are still headline news.

The conflict has never been resolved and I might be the only Jewish woman to have lost

the Six-Day War and witnessed the onset of Israeli occupation from a Palestinian perspective.

My first book, *Scrapbook of a Taos Hippie*, documents the counterculture in Northern New Mexico. Wish I still had my apartment on Avenue A. The furnishings sure would be worth a lot of dough! It would be great if you could read this book and share it with others.

It is a historical memoir— lots of personal stories wrapped into sharing the history while confronting the myths that most Jewish-Americans were weaned on

(book is available as print or Ebook on Amazon)"

Hi "Iris, say hello back to Faisal. What is he doing in Buffalo? What are you doing in Taos, one of my old haunting grounds? My friends Peter Rabbit and Annie MacNaughton lived there — I was World Heavyweight Poetry Champion one year at this great event they put on. We filmed in the Taos pueblo. And I re-met Ben Morea there, peyote drummer and ex-troublemaker at 2nd and St. Marks Place. He was briefly Most Wanted by the FBI. Gem's Spa is gone — it closed this year! The place has no charm for me now. As for NY, I remember our passing of keys and leaving. I remember the apartment well: there were many late night discussions, marijuana, acid. I remember Peter Schjeldahl stumbling in one night saying: "Can I stay here? I just ate a chicken full of hashish and I can't remember where I live." He was later art critic for *The New Yorker* for a million years — and still is! I have vivid memories of the Lower East Side, three formative years 1967-1970. There were pushcarts on Avenue C I photographed from the window. I think some of these real or slightly fictionalized details are in *The Life and Times of an Involuntary Genius* I wrote at 23. Chutzpah! I'll order your book today. Andrei"

* * *

This summer I've been listening to Miles Davis
It's been a choice, but also kind of a necessary salvation
This music I've listened to for decades
Is now going deeper, the fusion era
This is the music that calms me
In this era of depradation and sickness
Of massive protests and anger
Of focus on the injustice inherent in this place

This music contains all that
And also, always, other swerves
Not without acknowledgment of madness
And a sense of humor, or rather wit —
To be alive despite it all

[July 27, 2020]

CANTO
SEIS

[Canto Seis begun July 27, 2020]

I think of how we treat the lives
Of other species
There's wisdom in the show
The play of life and death
The act, the interaction
Daily, the effort for food, shelter
And the pursuit, the fight
The violence of survival

Indigenous people kill
In the recognition of their own death
They kill for food
Responsible for their economy
Within a small group

I think of how my matter will go
Into other forms of matter at my going
That's all it is
I am lucky to have this matter
For this time, to have consciousness

* * *

I wanted to see some sunlight
On a few piled cinderblocks
But by the time I could get back there
The sun had shifted
There are 10 of them, some quite new
Others older, a bit battered
Four are stacked horizontally
One lies on another at an angle
Plants grow through the exposed
Holes of three of them

* * *

Under the Horror Dome the poets soothe
by moving the camera now hyperclose now far
so multiplying the mysteries

67

why does the stock market for instance keep
going up while a wave of the miserably poor
are taking back the city they lost to tourists

why does the polis take these blows in stride
we live now in the technicolor version
of my black and white commie childhood

blissful in its way under the curtain of rain
outside the window of the ancient classroom
the drone of history bent to ideology

do we know too much or too little do we live
well or are we inside charlie kaufman's 700-page novel
Antkind, a book written by the rain of words in the head
of a man truthful in his affections and weakness
under attack by pronouns but capable of love, if truth

did not get in the way like a vertical Berlin Wall in Brooklyn
where language flourished once like poverty or madness
and wrote itself out in an ungendered lump of memes

* * *

The stone face smiles
The eyes alive
Smile embedded in
Permanent look
Morning sun
Hits left side of chin
Nose
Skull
Hair
Other factures also gleam
Right cheek
Eye sockets
A morning idol
After yoga
Dedication to

A free mind
Again
Let your heart
Guide you
They say

Last night
A Love Festival
On TV
Long-ago
Heightened bliss
In sacred space
Places for each
Sun in faces
Even when chill
Performances
Intimate
Unique in time
Resplendent

[9/8/20]

* * *

Crazy it's September

Today is the first day of Autumn
Not the date
But the crisp cold in the air
Bright light that stays outside
Inside is music and the desire
For a life, pundits claim
We're on the brink of something
Can anyone, can we, find a life anymore?
Is everything so changed
We won't find our way again?
It seems certain there is no
Going back, is there ever?

* * *

69

These are the high holy days
We are supposed to feel joy
Within the sorrow and
These days must be
Filled with dance and joy and love
How is that possible now?
The Hasidim taught that
But their tradition has been
Led astray, as are most

I can't really believe in a god
Anyway, some external force
To pray to, though I often
Feel the impulse, frustration
And inability, a psychological
Pressure to ask for help

But I'm on a different path
One that sees us animals
Or aspiring to be as pure
As our animal nature
With the discipline to cause
As little pain as possible
To think (or not to think)
Beyond the self

[9/19/20]

* * *

if i am the CEO of my own person
or at least the echo of my person
the executive cannot be among the resigned
thus with any executive
of a self a company or a nation
the CEO or the echo cannot be allowed to say
"it is what it is"
executive power in any form is authorized
to make what it is into what it is not

70

that is the definition of power
the struggle of executive power is with rhetoric only
especially the automated rhetoric of the medium or media
the codified grammar of the material logic
which is in any case only thickly layered subjectivities
so what is political poetry?
it is the gift of articulation the alms of the articulate
to the inarticulate the implied begging
delicately unallowed to humiliate itself
or au contraire rhetoric responding to loud
articulated demands
that refuse to be clothed in begging
which are already executive
if i am the CEO or echo of myself
i cannot say it is what it is

Covid is socialism
we are flattened by equality in misery
flat exceptionalism does not exist
self is denied agency
it strips the executive of all freedom
except death on the glass a squished bug
that was grey socialism in my youth
the only exit was art or suicide
which are the same entity stripped of power

* * *

Diane dead
Was trying to be in touch
Trying to reach her
Consistently including
Recently when we were
Organizing a reading
And wanted to read her work
We did

Anne read from "Rant"
And I read "Revolutionary Letter #39"
About dropping acid in Tompkins Square

Then going to the Museum of Natural History
The next day and seeing all the displays of animals
As historical artifacts of vanished species
On a smooth, plastic planet

Another dear poet friend is in hospice
That dire moment when communication is no longer
Possible, we listen to music, read poetry
"New ones coming as the old ones go," the song says
"Everything's moving here but much too slowly
A little bit quicker and we might have time
To say 'How do you do?' before we're left behind"

    i.m. Diane di Prima 25 October 2020

[10/27/20]

* * *

After a week of hitchhiking with Alice from New York to San Francisco
we went to Diane di Prima's house in the Haight to sleep (at her invitation).
We were beat, but before we could crash she made us collate
The Floating Bear along with 10 other communards. We earned
our sleep. And that was as they say the beginning of years hitching
from the Russian River to Diane's house in Tamales Bay on our way
to San Francisco making sure each time that we arrived around dinnertime,
Diane being the extraordinary cook that she was always welcoming us
with fresh food her fisherman friend brought that day from the Bay.
She cooked tender fish and crustaceans with sauces of her own invention
over handmade pasta and arugula (of which few had heard in 1975) salads
that we, Pat Nolan, Jeffrey Miller, sometimes Alice and Hunce,
ate amid thousands of books on practical magic, cartomancy, alchemy,
   homeopathy, poetry,
and vials of herbal medicine and other secret arts on floor to ceiling shelves.
I was also in love with Diane's grace and loose robes and saris,
and Hunce was in love with her preteen son Alex to whom
he dedicated a vast poem that Diane advised him to keep to himself.
Jeffrey loved her beauty and her food and he was often lost before the window
listening to the waves of the Bay for something we later knew were his ashes.
Full of goddess energy and seafood witchcraft we went on to San Francisco

to be terrible young poets with verses full of love and magic touched by di Prima. She was di Prima, the first, and Diana, the huntress and protector of youth.

[10/29/20]

* * *

I want to reach out to friends
Overwhelmed by emails
Asking me to call voters
I have called voters, mailed
Postcards and letters, trying
To get people motivated
This time, 77 million have
Already voted, seems to be
A surge to stem the idiocy,
The cruelty and violence

Today is Saturday
The elections are on Tuesday
"Let us raise a standard
To which the wise and honest
Can repair, the event
Is in the hand of God"

[10/31/20]

* * *

Today is Sunday, November 1st
The elections are in two days
Today *The New York Times* had
A section of the Sunday Review titled
"What Have We Lost?" There
Were some interesting answers:

Our Faith

"Today the greatest threat I perceive to America's national security isn't from Qaeda terrorists, Russian cyberattacks or Chinese missiles. As I see it, it's from Trump's re-election." — Nicholas Kristof

73

The World

"With the election of Donald Trump, America... put the most powerful country in the world under the control of a lying, grifting, shady carnival-conductor.... His entire life was a game of smoke and mirrors, double talk and double-dealing." — Charles M. Blow

"A second Trump term of erratic American belligerence meeting growing Chinese assertiveness would be pregnant with the possibility of violence." — Roger Cohen

"How useful is America as an ally when the president suggests that he might not defend European nations because, in his judgment, they don't spend enough on NATO?" — Paul Krugman

Culture

"Since Election Day 2016, writers, artists and critics have wondered what many forms of cultural production — novels, fine art, theater, fashion — mean 'in the age of Trump.' It's a cliché — one I know I've used — about the reorientation of almost everything around the monstrous fact of the Trump presidency." — Michelle Goldberg

[11/1/20]

* * *

Today, there's a party in Philly
It's in the political process
It is proceeding as it is supposed to
It ain't over yet
But Philly is dancing a dance we all
(yes, "we all" in their heart of hearts)
Approve and dance to, too

It's a powerful moment
When the voting system can more or less
Work, when each vote has an

Undeniable power
One of the few times citizens can exert influence
Directly in the public sphere
(jury duty another)

[11/6/20]

Yes, the Philadelphia Party is a good avant-garde party
It is happening now on TV before the Philly votes are in.
If I was in Philly and I'm not because I'm in Brooklyn
I would hope to be sober enough by the time we count
so I could pick up another celebrant to dance with.
This is my view as to what parties are for: dance even
if the Republic was saved which as of now is still only on TV.
Seventy million people voted for an autocrat so let's sober up
for a minute: seventy million Americans have a death wish
because brutal history resurfaces. Take it from a veteran
of planet earth who won't go to Mars with musk but has
been to muskova the russian planet and saw happy smiles
over bitter hearts in the planet of the utopian state party.
Are there still people or just children of television,
Images of what the producers would like to sell ads for?

[11/6/20]

CANTO
SIETE

[Canto Siete begun 12/14/20]

In the lump of melted time December 2020 the year of public
and private misery we make a gymnastic effort to see or walk.
Sight is still only screens with higher resolution and reality
more blurred. The republic appears steady on shaking old man's
legs but this may be virtual hope served to prisoners like a turkey
on a false thanksgiving. Vaccination haunts the world like
communism once did a utopia that is still only reporting on TV.
Before when billions of us competed for attention we found
it soothingly impossible to tell what anyone was doing if there
was no news of them at their "group activities"
as we called it in the schools that have long ago ceased existing.
Now everything is global. There is, we hope, a new "most powerful
man in the world" and billions of us will be vaccinated. Our whole
bioform makes news like one or a small group did when the spotlight
of the camera was choosing them. The only choice of a particular
distinction now resides in the (not insignificant number of) people
who believe that the vaccine carries 5G instructions to the bioform
to reveal what? Sexual differences? Those too have long ceased
to be of any import to the bodies we now hope not to drag to clinics.
You have nice breasts? Forget it, nobody's looking. Nice clothes? Ditto.
If you felt wanted or wanted someone once, the impetus has vanished.
After the last war those who hadn't died decided to do so intensely.
After this war I fear that all the living will be done by virtual bodies.
Our own bodies locked up so long will be slabs of flattened meat with tics.
I am otherwise an optimist, my optimism reserved for virtual people
I don't feel a thing about. As David Franks said, "things are so bad I dream
About masturbating," Things are so good I dream that plastic pixels might.

[12/14/20]

* * *

I dream about a togetherness
I dream of finding my people
I dream of helping someone unpack
I dream of touching someone on the shoulder

A little water pours from the pot
Before the coffee gushes out
We are starting the day
As soon we will be starting the year

What year will this be?
What sound will it have?

* * *

Last year started out optimistically
The name of the year in French
Was homophone to
Someone saying "Wine, wine"
It sounded like a celebration
But turned into a *cri de coeur*
Then ended in responsibility
The striving to be sensible
When everything is collapsing

[12/28/20]

"I" tweeted "Impossible to say 'I' in the extended provisional"
it is december 28 2020 the TV says "light at the end of the tunnel"
It is still december 2020—
my mother almost a century old the light flickers
at the end of the tunnel the light is exhausted it flickers

nothing is over "until the fat lady sings"
but my mother all bones and skin a little thing
passed from hand to hand a light thing
last night from nursing home to emergency
positive for Covid once a hurricane-mother

so back where we started at the origin
the tunnel of the poem the flickering light
of our selves drowned in the flickering "we"

just waiting for the call

Yesterday you said "I saw Lenin's tea cup" in Finland
on the phone from your car driving in upstate New York
I thought you said "Lenin's cap"
the iconic cap he bought in Sweden

today on my way back from taking Covid test
in Brooklyn I thought of Lenin's tea cup and saw him
taking a sip from it in his cap

and on the steps of a brownstone was this

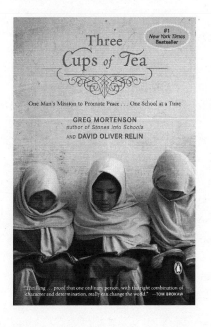

Three cups of tea: you, Lenin and me

Negative

still waiting for a call from Florida

12.30.2020 (geography)

* * *

Mother still kicking into 2021
Driving the nurses crazy with her crying
She must be Stalin's wife somebody said

Social workers practice calm voice before lying
About everything just like the president
They are trying to find a bed for mother but cannot
Decide whether to give it to her or curl in it and die
Themselves instead it's all the same

It's all the same is something I thought I'd never say

Somehow it isn't because it cannot, but do birds
Think these things? Do ducklings like alligator babies?
Quit being cute and start looking for food as soon as they can?
Nothing is the same when you hunt for food.
An orange is not a chicken Pittsburgh is not Mt. Hood.

I am too unmoored to raze the capitals on every line.

* * *

2021 and my mother is different
We all are, but she is more so
Living her own way, happy to have
Others around, they come and go
Movement through the house
Though deadened by the wily virus
Continues, flux of desire and work

So strange to live surrounded
In the clutches of this thing
No one really understands
Half living half not
Is that what we too have become?

Reading of those in prison and whether
Poetry has any penetration there
We know it does, we've written
To, written with, people *in carcere*
The question: are we all *in carcere*
No, not that way, certainly
But in another way
Are we fooling ourselves to ask?

[1/5/2021]

* * *

Today was a day that left me
Disoriented and feeling sick.
First we learned that Rev. Warnock
Had won in Georgia. Woo-hoo!
But what about Ossoff? Still
No result. Then I took my mom
To two doctors. She seemed
Very tired and out of sorts.
She was in pain, and I wanted
To alleviate her pain. We had to
Navigate through various public
Spaces, including a hospital,
Which I did not relish, for her
Sake, but her cardiologist had
Asked her to come in this time.
We wore plastic face shields
In addition to masks and worked
Our way through the challenges.

Finally, we got home and someone
Had the TV on, and we saw what
Was happening at the Capitol.
Proud Boys and others like them
Had stormed the Capitol building
Where Senators were attempting
To ratify the presidential election.

The images of civilians forcing
Their way in and battling
Guards inside the Capitol
Were deeply disturbing, whatever
One's thoughts on the presidency.

After walking home in the cold
(something I like to do, a break
In the day when I can be alone)
I had a terrible headache and felt
I might be coming down with
Something. I took a Tylenol and a
Bath and went to the basement
To hear Isaac and Oliver and Justin
Playing and started to feel a little
Better. Heard from someone
In Georgia who wrote, "Together
we helped to effect real positive change.
Don't y'all let today's hooliganism
in the Nation's capital diminish that."

And I came upstairs and had
A drink and watched some films
Oliver and Isaac had made years
Ago in school and on a trip we
All took together, and then
This show I really like about
Lawrence Durrell and his family
Living on the island of Corfu
In the 1930s... and then I ate
And listened to Ryuichi
Sakamoto and then I wrote...

[1/7/21]

* * *

Second day in the hospital
With my mom with shingles

84

Around her left eye
They are doing tests
Making sure it is not
Going to her brain

On Wednesday she started
Having trouble walking
And on Thursday stopped
And stopped speaking
She seemed a person asleep
Couldn't formulate words
Could not take solid food
Could not walk or bend
Her body to sit

Saturday we brought her
To Mount Sinai
And they began to hydrate
Observe and test
Now, Sunday, winter light
Strikes architecture, striking
Feature of this place, immense
Atrium evoking space of spirit
And eventual path upward
Exteriors too fraught with
Thought given to design
And peacefulness

Taking care of someone
The ultimate philanthropy

[1/10/21, MOUNT SINAI]

* * *

"Sad-Eyed Lady of the Lowlands"
In my ears, years of warmth and togetherness
In my eyes, the knowledge Aischylos
Promised us in my heart

85

I feel it there
But I wouldn't call it anything
It's the slow, steady revolving of the universe
The guitar jangles its rhythm quietly
The drums puncture images

The planet could keep itself together
If we weren't so intent on fucking things up
Let's not, let's try to protect
Things, I think that is possible
The people here, in this hospital
Are all trying to help
People get better, to feel better
There is a willful humanity
On display everywhere everyday
That can surpass the other levels

[1/11/21, MOUNT SINAI]

* * *

"The ghost of electricity howls in the bones of her face"

* * *

We twin here in the waiting for what we don't know
poetry/song generates warmth from friend to friend
solid oak bars of yesteryear leather seats fireplace
our mothers and fathers sat here before us in New York
and before that in vaulted wine cellars buried in snow
where Cossacks come to drink with the Jews keeping
the taverns. In the Spring they make pogrom and kill us.

The Cossacks took the U.S. Capitol in a cloud of whiskey,
fat bellies, horns, fur, and the moth-eaten flags
of one century ago like every other time the taste of blood
drives the masses crazy with its dense imaginary causes
for the world's ills. We poets note the civilized plazas

and the kindness of caring as the walls shake and glass shatters.
Under the circumstances writing is heroic.

Our mothers lived that century between Cossacks,
lived long enough for us to forget the horrors they bracket.
We honor them for surviving and for making us.
In the end all the fundamental questions have obvious answers.

* * *

in the ruddy quarrelous New World
and that is the ocean between

* * *

Airbnb is reviewing its bookings in the DC area
Ahead of next week's inauguration
Let's inaugurate something
Something is brewing

[1/12/21, Mount Sinai]

* * *

Listening to Ron Padgett talking about Joe Brainard:
Ron is relating how, when Joe decided that the art school
In Dayton, Ohio, where he was on a full scholarship in 1960,
Was not right for him, and NYC, which he had visited and loved,
Was right for him, he made up a lie that his father had cancer,
So that the school would feel it was okay for him to forego
His scholarship. Ron said that the only times Joe would lie
Would be when he thought that telling the truth might
Hurt someone's feelings, and he didn't want to hurt
The feelings of the art school he was not at home at.

Joe found a storefront on East 6th Street, just off
Cooper Square, the rent was cheap, at the turn of the year
Ted Berrigan showed up from Tulsa, because he decided
If Ron and Joe were moving to NY, he was too, and started
Sharing the storefront apartment with Joe, replicating

87

Picasso and Max Jacob, with Joe painting all day and sleeping
At night, and Ted sleeping during the day and writing and
Walking the streets at night, Joe, during this period, met
Joe LeSueur, who enlightened him as to his sexuality

Joe said, "If you painted a tree the way it looks,
No one would believe you."

[1/13/21, Mount Sinai]

*　*　*

An epic day!
The president has been impeached for the second time!
With only a week until the inauguration

[1/13/21, Mount Sinai]

*　*　*

I love that Nancy Pelosi wore the same dress
To both impeachments!! I don't love everything
She does, but she's been a bulwark against
The most egregious bullshit, and she's got style!

[1/14/21, Mount Sinai]

*　*　*

I'm in Central Park as the sun
Is getting low
There's still time though
In this winter afternoon
One of my biggest thrills
Is stepping off the path
Onto the earth underneath
A giant tree
It's winter so I'm not sure
But I'm going to say a giant oak

In fact, there are some stragglers
Leaves still clinging to
Branches up there that
Look like oak leaves

[1/14/21, Mount Sinai]

* * *

"The grimace of freedom shining down on me
Like a shingle dripping raindrops"

Lewis Warsh, *Blue Heaven*
i.m. 15 November 2020

* * *

In 1967 Alice and I stayed with Lewis and Allegra in Harlem
we knocked on the door
of the apartment in Harlem the door was open
we beheld Lewis sitting on a chair with Allegra in his lap
both of them naked and he inside her
not moving just sitting there young and beautiful
Lewis turned his head to us fresh from Detroit two kids
with all our worldly goods wrapped in two sleeping bags
"Welcome," Lewis said, "your room is down the hall"
We put our things down unrolled the sleeping bags
And considered our position: we were tired from hitchhiking
for two days hungry thirsty but not in the least sleepy
facing the dilemma of provincials arrived at last in the great city
of art and poetry at the place of a famous poet
we had brought a present for – a black T-shirt that said
"POETRY IS REVOLUTION" in red letters a Detroit anarchist item
but nothing for his girlfriend Allegra the most beautiful woman
I had ever seen – in fact I believe that I had met her the year before
at St. Mark's Church when Lewis invited us to stay when we returned.
In New York one year later – our dilemma was, in addition
to the single present – one T-shirt – the fact that our hosts were naked
and locked in sexual embrace as if posing for a painting

which had it been painted by let's say Alex Katz or Larry Rivers
would have been iconic of the whole epoch and hanging at MoMA
but even so burnt in my memory they sit two young bodies
poets beautiful at the crossroads between the 1967 Summer of Love
and the year of troubles and darkness 1968 –

our hunger won over our awkwardness
we left to find food and passed again the love-locked couple
posing for eternity
I lay the T-shirt on the floor in front of the love chair
and off into the breeze of Harlem summer night we went to find food
two white kids on the live all-Black street pumping blood and music –
at the bodega on the corner full of young men and women smoking
menthol cigarettes – I slipped a can of baked beans
– we had no money — under Alice's embroidered Mexican skirt
and left unobserved I believed two long-haired white kids
who had just stolen food because they were hungry and invincible —

back at the apartment Lewis and Allegra still in the chair inside one another
turned to see us come in smiling –
but Lewis wore the T-shirt we had brought him "POETRY IS
    REVOLUTION."

"We have beans" I said triumphantly

Later that night Allegra wore the shirt and we all ate the stolen beans

I will go back to Harlem now on January 26, 2021, to be vaccinated for Covid

Against the plague
ages of history stories new people lovers children
and now Lewis is no more
I wonder what became of Allegra

For Lewis Warsh (1944-2020)

* * *

Suspense is your name America January 18, 2021,
You are the dog that won't obey when we whistle.

Your dog Whistler is almost gone but you still hear him
Whistling "Dixie" in his tower of meat and stupidity
Diseased dismembered distraught he still whistles
But you only hear him in one ear because in your other
Ear you hear us the enemy of the raving lunatic
In the emptying tower of power with whom we have
In common only a disease that explains your mangy fur America
You are a place with a rotten sense of humor America
Your ruddy common sense has abandoned millions of your people
America land of struggle violence and cauldron of boiling snakes.
It looks like differences made a mighty strange mutt America.
Two days to go before the mad whistler is gone, and one century
Before the soup snake simmers down to a tolerable broth
We the new whistlers we will not tolerate for long because we are
A capricious and demanding people who have in common
the disease of exceptionalism destiny and the worship of stupidity.

* * *

"It is the final full day of the Trump administration." – *NY Times*, 1/19/21

* * *

Incredible, that we have his claws out from our backs
Maybe not permanently, but for now
There are so many images of care
Antidote to terrible motif of slaughter and uncaring faces
A story I'm reading about a family composed
Of people who need each other not born into
But found, founded, the need in another
The hope and longing, felt that, and moved
Into a track that could bring that support

A card that says someone misses someone
They long "to dance again the whirling of life"
Photograph of a couple holding each other
In preparation of some recorded happiness
One is not sure one could reach that one

[1/19/21]

91

* * *

Here's to tomorrow —
May it feel like when Obama was first elected
The difference being that was an election
This is an inauguration
Rarely has an inauguration felt so contested
The last one something like it was Bush 2
Where the contest dragged on so long
Through chads and illegal challenges and defenses
(beyond the unique idiocy of the Electoral College
Which I have wanted abolished for decades)
Let's see...

[1/19/21]

* * *

In two hours, Joe Biden will be inaugurated, and this nightmare will be over.

[1/20/21]

* * *

It's Mozart's birthday again.
That means we've been working
On this epic for exactly one year.
You and I both know epics take
More than a year, more than
A couple of years. Maybe multiple
Years to craft something worthy
Of the name epic?

But the miracle is that I'm sitting
Looking out the window on a sunny
Late January day, the shadows
Evocative of painting and also
Nothing, themselves, the light

92

And shapes on rooftops, chimneys,
Elevator and stair housings,
Distant architectural embellishment,
All exist as themselves, for nothing,
For this moment.

And I'm listening to Mozart's violin.
The actual violin he owned and played.
That is the miracle. The radio
Is bringing me his *Violin Concerto
No. 4 in D, K. 218*, played by
Les Musiciens du Louvre,
Christoph Koncz, conductor,
Christoph Koncz, violin.

22 minutes, 46 seconds,
In which Mozart himself,
His violin, is playing, and
Anyone can hear it.

[1/27/21]

* * *

What has happened in a year?

CANTO
OCHO

Making the World

The Museum der Kulturen Basel and
The Kunstmuseum Basel pool their resources:
Deities and Demons locked in combat
The Titanomachy of Greek mythology
The voyage of the soul
The soul of a dying person
The prospect of admission to
One of several paradises
While the Olympian gods transform Psyche
Into one of their own
Approachable and responsive Ganesha
Venus and Amor, divine ambassadors
Shiva shines unrivaled while
12-year-old Jesus confounds conventional wisdom

An empty throne
An empty chair during circumcision
Held for the prophet Elijah
The sun and the moon stand still for a day
Angels and Saints worship the word not God

[1/31/21]

* * *

"The urgent need to talk was manifest."
—Joseph Beuys, 1969

* * *

Pissarro took an active interest in anarchism
He did not wish his pictures to be read
As visualizations of a political program
Still, core ideas of anarchism resonate

* * *

Sophie Taeuber-Arp worked in textiles,
Beads, puppet theater, costumes, murals,
Furniture, architecture, graphic design,
Painting, drawing, sculpture and relief

Her characteristic lucid yet animated
Formal idiom is recognizable

The lively interplay of equilibrium
and motion

Her face familiar to many
Thanks to its presence on the

Swiss 50 franc note

[1/31/21]

* * *

She has been included in every day
The day is very cold and very sunny
It is the winter sun of memories
Of winter and of sun, and my mother
Does not see it or feel the cold

I brought her to the window today
To see if she might like to feel it
But she wanted to return to the sofa
The nearest place to sit seems best
Eating she has taken to, always a sign
Of healing, sometimes she puts
Her hands over her eyes, a healing
Gesture, it does help

The days move slowly, their light
Palpable, and Oliver has flown
Through night back in time
To California, where warmer
Weather awaits him, and us

[1/31/21]

Music and art comfort you, friend.
As do the ones you love and care for.
You are a much better person than I.
In my youth I chased dreams and talked,
talked to anyone but to women mostly.
I had at my core a need to tell my distant
mother stories that to her were noise
or a murmur, as they must have sounded
also to the row of caretakers who fed
and bathed me but had little use for my words.
The words they needed I didn't have:
Meat at the store on Tuesday, flour on Friday.
A man in a trenchcoat is asking questions.
I didn't know those questions or when
the meat and flour might show up.
The words I knew were not from our world.
I told stories about being in the China of my mind.
I told about the books I read. I once said
to the policeman's wife: I invented the telephone
at King Arthur's court. I told stories from books.
I felt good lying on the stone porch in the sun
thinking up stories and I fell asleep telling myself
adventures until one day the sun burnt me to a crisp.
I said "Goddam you sun!" A shadow stood above me
and I sat up still cursing, I was four or five years old,
and the shadow blotted out the sun and a hand
slapped my face. "Never say that about the sun!"
said the policeman's wife. A large and mostly kind
woman she was at heart a pagan. To insult the sun
was the greatest crime, a pre-Christian sin. And
she meant it. And I learned my lesson. I will never
curse the sun again. *Au contraire*, I greet it
like Frank O'Hara and I am sure to bless it when it shines.
Still I can use more sun lotion to be frank.
So to this age I came, my friend, a lover of books,
a polite sun worshipper, though a trouble-maker
in my youth when I wanted the world to hear me talk.

I am a poet I told the sun one day, and I must talk
to people! I love poets, sun! I must meet them all.
This week poets I loved died: Lewis Warsh, Dick Gallup,
Clayton Eshelman. Lewis I knew it seems forever
in my new land in those fabled Sixties, and he was
kind to me, a generous soul. Dick Gallup, one of the Tulsa
cowboys who took over the 60s New York poetry scene,
along with Ted Berrigan, Ron Padgett and Joe Brainard,
friend also and long gone now.
Dick was a dear friend in New York where he invited
Alice and me for dinner, just like grownups did. We ate
spaghetti and met Peter Schjeldahl, who waited up all night
for his first story about art in the *NY Times* Sunday magazine.
I hung out with Dick in Monte Rio, California, on the Russian River
and then San Francisco where he drove a cab, smoked cigarettes,
and wrote poetry he showed me reluctantly one night
when we drove in his cab and talked and talked.
Ah, poets, quit dying, you break my heart.
Clayton Eshleman published one of my first poems in English.
I was 20 and I wrote "with a mask of English." Clayton
printed one in his magazine, *Caterpillar*. Another was published
by Anne Waldman in *The World* and another in *El Corno Emplumado*,
in Mexico City, Margaret Randall's quarterly.
I was 20 years old and I was talking to my contemporaries.
I love you poets, you are my comfort, quit dying please.

In the meantime The Republic wobbles, every one of our well
functioning institutions seeded with fascist saboteurs.
I feel that we are living through the slow roll-out
of a mass extinction of humans in the ongoing Plague.
My burst of optimism when we elected Biden/Harris is flickering
like the flame of a candle about to go out.
"Dying with Others" is no longer a metaphor.
The other bioforms were here before the arrogant bipeds came
and they will be here long after we are gone.

i.m. Dick Gallup 27 January 2021
i.m. Clayton Eshleman 30 January 2021

[1/31/21]

* * *

Franz Schubert was born on this date in 1797.
He died 31 years later, having packed into that
Short time on earth a fantastic number of
Songs, symphonies, operas, piano music,
Including the *Wanderer Fantasy*, which we heard
On the radio while driving through the snow
To my parents' house, a performance by
Seong-Jin Cho with the English Chamber
Orchestra, conducted by Paul Goodwin.

Much earlier in the day, we had heard
The same orchestra and conductor
In a performance, on the radio, of
Edward Elgar's *Serenade in E Minor*.

[1/31/21]

* * *

Today is my parents' 63rd wedding anniversary;
He is 93, she is 92. We are in the midst
Of one of the worst blizzards in recent memory.

[2/1/21]

* * *

Evan Rachel Wood
Has always been one of my favorite
Actresses
She has pushed the limits
Thirteen
Did you see it?
One of those supposedly "pop"
Movies
Its main audience was mothers
Who brought their 13-year-old

Daughters
That by their artistry
Transcend
Category
Largely through Evan's
Empathetic, subtle
Training on this
Girl

I wonder what Holly Hunter's thinking
About this news of Evan's suffering
I am breathing in this suffering
And trying to breathe out healing balm

[2/2-3/21]

* * *

We went to a new doctor today

* * *

"Oh my sweet thing, oh my honey thighs,
Give me your troubles, I'll keep them with mine"
(PJ Harvey)

* * *

so time rolls and rolls
children and dogs in the first great snow of early february 2021
snowballs flying with the joy of Brueghel winters
on the lake we saw a bird that was not a goose or duck
or the pair of swans that geese and ducks keep a respectable
distance from as if they were mean gods very much taken by their grace
though god knows they could use a bath their ballerina necks
are filthy whereas the ducks are always beaking themselves clean

the new bird with long brown webbed feet and white beak
that after much googling we saw was the american coot

similar to the eurasian coot but honestly
if I was asked to tell the difference I would have to catch one
to look at its tail feathers
its minute description having been sketched by a naturalist in 1806
a talented observer who doubtlessly held a dead coot —

don't you just love those 19th century naturalists,
darwin and co who made those marvelous drawings
even audubon bought his birds from the french market
in new orleans and he often traded drawings of birds
for other birds at that tropical baroque market

the new world was a gift to the bourgeois table
and a gift to john james audubon
and it continues to be a gift this easter in the snow
when it displays for us the american coot

humans are becoming pallid and not new and all
i pass these humble bundles on their health walks
and cannot tell men from women or whatever lives
in those bundles of cloth and fur
pandemic beings of the future
not a coot among them though maybe geese and swans
masked and disguised holding a flickering sense of self within

the day when we shed this pandemic will be a riot
of great emerging birds for audubon to illustrate

this is park slope in february '21 we vote and demonstrate
we do not kill our models to draw their differences

[2/4/20]

* * *

« IL S'ESSAIE À VIVRE »

* * *

Dream:

We are driving through London. We are using a GPS, which is taking us over bridges and down dark avenues. We seem to be getting where we are going. Are we heading out of town? It's not entirely clear. Eventually, we arrive at a large building, an older loft building in a somewhat modern, industrial part of town. We get out of the car and go inside. There we find a large loft-like entry space with a few people scattered around. It feels like a party, but turns out to be more like an institute of studies. Food is prepared for the people there and, upstairs, there are separate work spaces. We are looking for a man who is somehow in charge of this place. He is about 40 years old, with dark hair, maybe of Indian descent. He knows us, but as we have neither called ahead nor made an appointment, he is not able to see us. He apologizes and disappears. We go upstairs and meet some other people, talk for a while, then decide to leave. The visit seems to have been unsuccessful, but on the other hand, we are on the search for something together. We get back into the car and drive away.

[2/12/21]

I am in a big house, a communal lodge of some sort, dedicated to the healing arts, yoga, herbs, not quite sure. I walk into one of the rooms where I have a flirtatious conversation with a young woman about the residence and its thermal baths. I open a door and there is a woman meditating in front of a wide window, next to a large square empty hot tub. My new friend is taking me to the dining hall to meet the leader, there are people seated already, and I know that we are in Oregon in the woods. Suddenly my first wife Alice, my second wife Laura, her sister Susan, my brother-in law Lloyd, and Laura's son Will are there, dressed in winter clothes. I feel just a bit awkward, but I introduce them to everyone I haven't yet met. My family is not all that friendly, they sit around stiffly as if I'm supposed to explain somehow why I'm there. I really don't know why they are so uptight, but I think once they warm up (it's snowing) and eat, they'll begin to improve à la hippie therapeutic model. Personally I would like to go to the room with the big window and the square hot tub, but now I can't, due to the presence of family. I wake up thinking: there were some people not there.

* It seems everyone is having these dreams

I think there are two kinds of money: money you have and money you owe. They are both commodities, but money you owe is more precious than money you have because more people care for you so that you'll pay them back. Likewise, there are two kinds of memory: one for remembering and one for forgetting. There are so many passwords to remember you fear forgetting, you entrust a machine with remembering your passwords, also phone numbers and pictures. When you begin to lose your memory, you ask the machine, but it turns out that the machine for remembering was really a machine for forgetting. The machine was forgetting for you all that you would have forgotten yourself without machines. So there are two kinds of machines, for remembering and for forgetting. You must remember which is which. It turns out that there are also two social systems that have two different penal systems. There is socialism which pays for imprisoning you and providing for you in prison, and capitalism, where you imprison yourself (because of pandemic panic) and you must provide for yourself. Socialism and capitalism succeed each other in imprisoning you because socialism uses resources to feed prisoners, while capitalism uses prison labor so that socialism can succeed it. Isn't it nice that we have two of everything except for the nose and the genital?

* * *

Chick is with Mozart.
To prove it, WQXR plays a suite
Of pieces by him from his last album,
Last year's *Plays*, which is a great title,
Especially for one's final offering.
It includes Mozart, Tom Jobim,
Bill Evans, Chopin, Monk, Stevie
Wonder and children's songs.
We hear him play
A Scarlatti sonata live in Paris.
Then, as if to accentuate the point,
They play a Mozart divertimento.

We should divert ourselves
From sad thoughts, they don't really
Exist, less get us anywhere
Well, we never get anywhere, that's okay
But the Italians know *divertente*
Means amusing, entertaining
That's what we should do
For others, for ourselves

Chick seemed to know that
He was of Italian descent
I always thought he was Latinx
I guess Italian *is* in a way
Lazio is the modern Latium
His nickname, Chick, I learned
Came from a grandma who
Called him "Cheeky" due to
His protuberant cheeks as a kid,
"Chick" being the hipper,
More streamlined, version

The young hipster moved to NYC
To study and, well, you know the rest
If you don't, I recommend a deep dive
Into Miles's fusion period, beginning
With *Bitches Brew*, then work your way
Back to *Filles de Kilimanjaro* and ahead
To *Live-Evil*, and beyond

   i.m. Chick Corea 9 February 2021

[2/13/21]

* * *

Dr. Zhivago is on television
We watch it from the beginning
And I remember seeing it with my mother
Close to when it came out

I remember the ending in the
Frozen house, how romantic
That image was
But I didn't remember the beginning

Did anyone ever tell you
Your father was a poet?

I realize it was believable
Because it looked like a film
From its time

Of course, the novel
Was of its time as well

Poetry is no more a vocation
Than good health

We wonder who is more
Beautiful, Julie Christie or
Omar Sharif? We think it's
Julie Christie, but Omar
Moves like a dancer. He
May have the best movement
In the movies since Errol Flynn.

Visually, the movie is somewhere
Between 007 and Bergman,
But closer to 007. We understand
The movies through their visuals,
Not through the words.
The words are incidental.

I brought you this:
It has a feature on young
Russian poets

Help! was made the same year
Maybe Richard Lester is
A better director than
David Lean

To a poet, she's very beautiful

Did you write some poetry?
Yes, quite a lot
Is it good?
Yes, I think so

He approved us
But for reasons which were subtle
Like his verse

I had the impertinence
To ask him
For a volume of his poems

And then we parted

I used to admire your poetry
I shouldn't admire it now
I should find it absurdly personal
The personal life is dead
In Russia

The private life is dead
For a man with any manhood

[2/13/21]

* * *

Mozartiana, Orchestral Suite No. 4 in G, opus 61

* * *

John Coltrane, *Transition* (recorded 1965, released posthumously, 1970)

* * *

Gluck, *Orfeo ed Euridice*

They sit in a field
Surrounded by daffodils
Smiling, looking, tumbling
Ostensibly they are posing
But in effect they are being
Nature as it affects their
Being together in this moment
Of their youth together

In that, they are primal
Reminders of how we animals
Are all together in a moment
Before it gets taken away
Or we choose to move
From it, but now
We feel a vibration
From the earth

We are sitting on it
You can see earth, and one
Is upside down, his head touches
Earth, waist bridges up
How can everyone be
The same age? Their long
Hair of their time, their jeans
And T-shirts symbols of an age

Uncertainty caught there
A moment ago
Forty-three years suddenly
Nothing, that perfect time
They are together, can they
Gather that? Make something
From it, someone, take time
To be free from it

[2/28/21]

CANTO NUEVE

"The Met Fifth Avenue and The Met Cloisters Closed
to the Public Today Due to Inclement Weather"
[February 1, 2021]

"And watch them fade out"
PJ Harvey ("The Wheel")

disasters haunt us
a panther haunts a jogger

from her foaming fangs
they rescue me
they dust me off for history

my friend said I think in french
otherwise I shop

shopping is thinking
but it wasn't always

in french or in esperanto
the mistral or the föhn

used to encourage suicide
among thinkers in europe

it is what happens when latin
is no longer spoken in the market

[3/4/21]

* * *

Hindu god Kubera chilling with the all-cool sign
With a human in Namaste pose
13th century Chennakesava Temple, Somanathapura, Karnataka, India
Namaste or Añjali Mudrā common in Hindu temple reliefs

There's a dude getting entwined in giant snakes
In a 7th century temple in Chhattisgarh
He pushes his palms together, delicate fingers too
Bows his head slightly to the right

[3/10/21]

* * *

the first true Spring day March 12 2021
I sit on a bench in Prospect Park in Brooklyn
radiant humans walk by pallid trembling shapes
snails out of their shells they have shed coats scarves
long johns sweaters those mounds of indistinct
black and grey hideout gear have been shed
to rejoice in the sun oh joy oh frolicking bodies

women and men exist
there are women and men in the world again
for a time I thought I had a pre-pandemic
dream of indistinct beings
for a year I lost their contours

I am not dreaming it is the first day
of true spring and I think how good
it is to sit on this bench in the sun
and how lucky I am to have this dream again

"Do you happen to be Jewish?" a bright boy asked me

I knew it being Friday the Lubavitchers
were fishing for souls and I would have said
as I had in Queens many times:
"yes but I'm dipped in shiksah"
"I am a buddhist in my last incarnation"
but this time it was spring and now I said
"Yes" and another boy appeared and asked
"Have you been bar mitzvahed?"
I said, "My mother gave me a Pobeda watch
with a black screen when I turned 13
but I never knew why."
And up came another sunny boy who asked:
"How old are you" I said: "Seventy-four."

And then a whole slew of boys appeared,
summoned by the first boy's cell-phone.
I told them about Romania and how
Israel bought me from the dictator of that country

at 20 years of age for $2,000 and that is how
I gained my freedom thanks to being Jewish,
but I am not religious I am agnostic,

and then the boy asked if they could properly
bar mitzvah me now and I said "Yes" and they shouted
with joy and tied the tefillin around my arm
and put a black cube on my head and I repeated
after them the Baruch Adonai Hamvorach
and suddenly the lot of boys there
started to dance and sing! They waved around me twice!

In Prospect Park on the first day of Spring March 12 2021
this 74-year-old guy became a Jewish man and one of the boys said
"Now the watch your mother gave you runs backwards
and you're 13!" No kidding, I felt it.
"As long as there is no second bris" I said.
They scattered laughing chirping birds in the springtime.

* * *

"That was quite sweet," the old guy (old like me)
sitting on the next bench said. "I was young once."
I heard his accent and asked. "Greek," he said,
"from Salonika, my family saved a Jewish family
during the war." And then we talked, we talked

a long time, about Greeks, Jews, and my friend
Nanos Valaoritis, who introduced Surrealism to Greece,
and then had to flee when the colonels came to power
in the 1970s, and "That's when I fled, too," my bench
neighbor said. "I had a Greek restaurant in Brooklyn,
but now for me happiness is to sit on this bench
for 40 minutes when the sun is out, to watch
young people go by." "And why," I said, "did you
not let these kids bar mitzvah you too, they would
have, even if you happen to not be a Jew?"
"Yes," he replied, "and then have to flee again
from the Lubavitchers when they find out
that I wasn't circumcised? No thanks, I think
I'll just stay here in the sun." The sun liked that.
I liked him too, the Spring, the kids, the ritual.

CANTO
DIEZ

"the experience of the divine encounters a force, not an individuality"
— Paul Veyne

quisque suos patimur manis
Vergil, *Aeneid*, book 6, line 743

Carl Philipp Emanuel Bach's *Cello Concerto*
Played by the Orchestra of the Age of Enlightenment

the grasshopper *Ingenuity*
powered by the microchip designed by Lucian Codrescu
my first son who at the age of 13 would not
come in to eat all day until he won the game
on the Commodore box in his secret room
we called it Stubbornness but it was *Perseverance*
the rover from whose belly jumped *Ingenuity* today
to the surface of Mars April 5 2021

to photograph the surface of the red planet
for the first time in human history
Mars is indeed red and its hills and valleys
are red and dense with the absence of presence
martian life is still here maybe in the vast ice ocean
under the red earth the human grasshopper *Ingenuity*
is already upsetting or bringing Enlightenment
to the martians who refuse to come in to eat until they finish
whatever they are doing under the ocean of red dirt

* * *

The deejay was saying they had listened to
Billie Holiday performing "What a Little Moonlight'll Do"
Live at Carnegie Hall (he said "Car-Nay-Gie" – you know
The guy's not from New York when he says "Car-Nay-Gie")
And then he said we'd listen to
Grover Washington Junior accompanied by
Billy Cobham, Ron Carter, et al
Performing a piece composed by Cobham
"Taurian Matador"

Monk's Time (Monk was on cover of *Time*)
Al Jarreau singing Al Green

The guys at the Mobil station
The inspection

* * *

George Floyd's face on murals flags posters
kind face in Spring justice flowers a good day
faux-ending for a four-year nightmare
spring flowers + justice = sprig of heart hope
if I was young say and knew nothing of history
I would be happy too but I am not I cannot
celebrate America's prisons they are full
yet flowers this Earth Day 2021 make happy dizzy head
a russian grandmother says everything has a name day
each tree cow chicken lilac has a day when they are
shown respect – no cow would step on a lilac bush
on its name day no chicken would carelessly lay an egg
so that a dog might step on it no cat would tangle with a dog
on the dog's name day you cannot be mean to me on my name day
and by "you" I mean flowers, and earth has a name day too
be good to the earth today don't dig it up don't throw seeds in it
do not swear using its name it is Earth Day and everything
on Earth has a name day

April 22, 2021

* * *

George Floyd, finally

His murderer sent down on three counts
On April 20, 2021, a jury of six whites and six blacks
Found him guilty of unintentional second-degree murder,
Third-degree murder, and second-degree manslaughter
Minnesota defines third-degree murder as
"depraved-heart murder," where an individual acts
With "depraved indifference" to human life

But what is justice to a dead man?

"We are the hurdles we leap to be ourselves"
Michael McClure

Came to S.F. to be a painter
But shifted gears under
Robert Duncan to study
Poetry at S.F. State instead
Gaining his B.A. in 1955

Not long after, he was present at
And participated in
One of the seminal moments
Of contemporary American poetry:
The reading at Six Gallery
On Friday, October 7, 1955, at 3119 Fillmore Street
With Ginsberg, Lamantia, Snyder and Whalen
McClure read "Point Lobos Animism" and "For the Death of 100 Whales"
Snyder, "A Berry Feast"
Whalen, "Plus Ça Change"
Ginsberg read "Howl"
For the first time in public

i.m. Michael McClure 4 May 2020

Jerry Slick, who got his B.A. 10 years after McClure,
Also went to State and soon after graduation
Co-founded The Great Society
A precursor to The Jefferson Airplane, Great Society
Featured Jerry's wife, Grace, who wrote "White Rabbit" in those early days
Great psychedelic anthem
Later under modulating circumstances

* * *

Three grand special exhibitions have been scheduled:
A retrospective of the art of Sophie Taeuber-Arp
A comprehensive presentation of the work of Kara Walker
And the first retrospective of the work of Camille Pissarro
In Switzerland in more than 60 years

Taeuber-Arp was a pioneer
Walker's works are displays of our hidden fears and prejudices
Pissarro ranks among the great facilitators and inspirers
An obsessive painter who lived for his work
Also a key figure in his intense and fruitful
Collaborative relationships with other artists
Some of them decades younger
He was a bridge from Courbet and Corot to
Monet, Cézanne, Seurat and Signac

[4/24/21]

* * *

Johann Sebastian Bach, *Concerto for Oboe, Strings and Continuo* (Arranged
by Andreas Tarkman from Cantata Music) – Performed by Albrecht Mayer
and English Concert – "Voices of Bach"

I'm enjoying concertos for solo instruments
This was never my favorite genre
I always preferred straight-up orchestral,
Vocal music, chamber music,
And yes, piano concertos
But now, for the first time, I'm really
Understanding concertos for other instruments
This is not entirely true
Many years ago, as a teenager
I loved Mozart's flute and oboe concertos
But Mozart was always a separate issue

[5/4/21]

* * *

What I really like
Is getting new poetry books in the mail
Today, I received *Swole* by Jerika Marchan
The Story of My Accident is Ours by Rachel Levitsky
Under the Sun by Rachel Levitsky

Facing You by Uche Nduka
Heaven is All Goodbyes by Tongo Eisen-Martin
and
Evergreen Review, Vol. 1, No. 2
"San Francisco Scene"
Copyright 1957
Editors: Barney Rosset and Donald Allen
Circulation and Business Manager: Fred Jordan
It includes an early publication of "Howl"
Kerouac's "October in the Railroad Earth"
Michael Rumaker's "The Desert"
Poems by Rexroth, Brother Antoninus,
Duncan, Ferlinghetti,
Spicer, Snyder, Whalen,
And this one by Michael McClure:

Night Words: The Ravishing

How beautiful things are in a beautiful room
At night
Without proportion
A black cat on a white spread
A black longhaired cat with a sensitive human face
A white robe hangs on the wall
Like a soft ghost
Without proportion
Songs flit through my head
The room is calm and still and cool
Blue gray stillness
Without proportion
The plants are alive
Giving of votive oxygen
To the benevolent pictures above them
Songs flit through my head
I am taken with insomnia
With ambrosial insomnia
And songs flit through my head
The room is softened
Things are without proportion
And I must sleep

Plus Photographs of Eight Poets
By Harry Redl

And it all came from the Insomniac Bookshop
In West Des Moines, Iowa

* * *

"Dartmouth Cheating Cases
Fault Use of Tech Tracking"

Tech is following us, retroactively
Determining what we did or didn't do
Isn't there a way we can judge our students
That doesn't require spying on them?

[*NY Times*, May 9, 2021]

* * *

In books live people we will never meet
how amazingly quiet they are when we don't read them
how tremendously alive they are when we do
how many things we will never use are in books
how many or few we use depends on how we read them
dresses we will never fit in we will never use
I also doubt that the anvil for shooing horses in Dumas
will ever leave the stables of Milady or her fleur-de-lys
though it is the most popular tattoo in New Orleans

CANTO
ONCE

So in an email of april 9 I am asked
"are you the Andre Codresco who wrote me a poem in 1967?"
in 1967 my english was primordial "the thing" and "do"

well yes who else codrescu's first public appearance
is in small letters one of those illegible psychedelic posters
by gary grimshaw advertising in big letters the MC5
"with french poet andre codresco"

MAITREY 2021: 24 HOURS IN APRIL 2021

April 9, 2021

Sent via form submission to Andrei Codrescu

NAME: Sharon Lowen

SUBJECT: I may have a poem you wrote me in feb 1967. If so let me know where to send a scanned copy for your archives

MESSAGE: The joy of COVID enforcing the opportunity to stay home and finally go through paper archives turns up a poem "For Sharon - I am a body made out of strings". It is by Andre Codresco, so perhaps it wasn't you? If by chance it is, I'd love to send it to you as these "blasts from the past" are sweet reminders of youth. It's possible we connected in Detroit or Ann Arbor. '67 is when I graduated Cass Tech. I live in India, came as a Fulbright scholar in '71, and have had a fulfilling career as a classical Indian dancer and part of moving the tradition forward over 47 years. best, Sharon Lowen

April 9, 2021

Dear Sharon, what an interesting find. I was just learning English around then. Not long ago, I was asked to write a poem for an anthology of Detroit poets, and I wrote "Detroit, City of Strings." To me, those strings of light were what I saw on LSD while I walked around Wayne State and the Detroit Art Museum. I must have been fresh off the strings of light when I wrote that, and it stayed with me.

Congratulations on your life-long dancing. Terrific dedication.

If you can scan or photograph it and send a copy, I would love to see it. Most of my archive is at Hill Memorial Library at LSU in Baton Rouge.

Wow! Time!

Thank you,
Andrei

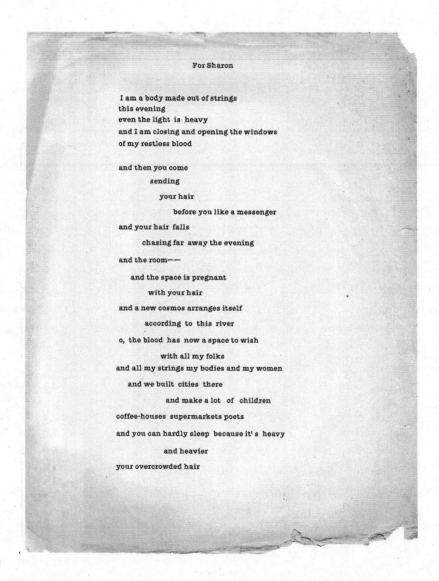

For Sharon

I am a body made out of strings
this evening
even the light is heavy
and I am closing and opening the windows
of my restless blood

and then you come
            sending

                your hair

                        before you like a messenger
and your hair falls

            chasing far away the evening

and the room——

        and the space is pregnant

            with your hair

and a new cosmos arranges itself

            according to this river

o, the blood has now a space to wish

            with all my folks
and all my strings my bodies and my women

        and we built cities there

                    and make a lot of children

coffee-houses supermarkets poets

and you can hardly sleep because it's heavy

            and heavier

your overcrowded hair

Dear Andrei,

I'm glad I valued this soap bubble of tender interaction as our lives crossed in Detroit. We seem to have shared an unconsummated intimacy as I was then, 1967, still like "Shakuntala, a flower whose fragrance none has tasted".

I scanned this to my archives/history file and saw a photo of me then which I'm also attaching, along with the poem. Wiki and Google shows the inevitable transformation of 54 years. Yes, wow, time.

kind regards,
Sharon

April 10, 2021

Dear Sharon: How extraordinary! You have had an amazing life and accomplished such marvelous arts. Your bio reads like a dream — the names of your practices and teachers alone make a hypnotic and beautiful sound. You are breathtakingly beautiful in that young picture, but it doesn't seem that time has had much power over you. Did you read *Maitreya*, (1933) a novel by Mircea Eliade about his first love in India? Not long ago, Maitreya, who is still alive I think, wrote her own book about that long ago affair. It was quite a different take — but she still looked amazing on the book jacket. Something about India — and dance.

The poem I wrote to you then must have been my first poem in English. I think I was a "French" poet then because that's how the name was first spelled in print — on one of those barely legible psychedelic posters by Gary Grimshaw, advertising the MC5 and a few minor acts, such as "French poet Andre Codresco." It is truly extraordinary that you still have the poem, which is a pure love poem of the sort one can write only at that age. Infallible instinct for unreachable muse, alas.

Thank you for making this an extraordinary day — it is like finally opening a door at the end (we hope) of the Pandemic Age — and seeing something incredibly beautiful there.

If you have a terrestrial address, I will send you my latest book of poetry so you can look inside poetry to see what time did there. Happy to report there are still love poems in there, but they are in a worldly whiskey-tempered voice (or so I'd like to think).

I will look at YouTube to see you dance.

Andrei

April 11, 2021

Dear Andrei,

Yes, I'm familiar with Maitreya, both versions. Your transition from your French spelling to Romanian lent to my doubting the Google results, but your website made it likely. Your "worldly whiskey-tempered voice" made me laugh out loud, thanks.

I embraced opportunities to serve as muse, until I understood the hubris of it. Remarkable that this was probably your first poem in English; remarkable that it was a pivotal moment in your wonderful poetic career; but most remarkable indeed is that it captures the sweetness of a pure love at that age. I think I actually continued to believe in that kind of love for far too long until I eventually understood that I should not trust my judgment and enjoy the uncomplicated freedoms of solo life, especially embedded in a traditional society like India's.

Thanks for bringing back memories of Gary Grimshaw and MC5. That was actually the height of a wonderful era for Detroit. The next year was the Detroit riots, I was in London with Julian Beck's Living Theatre at the Roundhouse after my first year at U of Mich, having created my own honors degree in Fine Arts and Humanities; first freshman elected to Student Government, and onward. I'm so happy our ships passed close in the night, and I preserved this unique capsule of our hearts in Feb '67.

Yes, without the pandemic, I might never have faced another dusty stack of papers and found this. I'd be delighted to read your latest book.

Sharon Lowen
New Delhi
India

warm regards,
Sharon

* * *

Every night, when we put my mom to bed,
I stay with her for a few minutes
I hold her hand and tell her to think about
Nice things so she can have nice dreams
I tell her to think about Sunny or Lulu,
Or Isaac and Oliver when they were little

Then I give her a kiss and she gives me one

I tell her I love her, and usually she says, "I love you"

Last night, she looked at me for a long time, smiling,
And said "Thank you" then, turning, said "Thank you,"
Again, "Even if I" she paused for a fraction of a second,
"faint" "You're not going to faint" I said

And then "Buona notte" "Buona notte"
"A domani" "A domani"
"Ti amo" "Anch'io, ti amo"

[5/21/21]

* * *

Péchés de vieillesse, Album de chaumière
Un profond sommeil - Un réveil en sursaut

We are listening to Rossini on the radio
These piano pieces are not as well-known as the operas
The titles (French above) would be

Sins of Old Age, Cottage Album
A Deep Sleep - A Wake-Up Call

I love the idea of Sins of Old Age!
We usually think of sinning as the province of the young!
And also, from our sleepy cottage —
A Wake-up Call!
Don't mope around!
Make the most of your time!
You are alive!

[5/24/21]

* * *

This morning I'm listening to
Chopin's *Nocturne No. 2* in E-flat, Op. 9 No. 2
Played by Angela Hewitt
Under the auspices of the Berlin Philharmonic
Sir Simon Rattle conducting

It's so soothing
I haven't appreciated Angela's playing yet
See? There is time for so many beautiful things
One hadn't realized were right there to be
Appreciated on a Tuesday morning before

The crush, listening to the radio at 8:34 a.m.
Having already meditated and discussed
About to return to Greek translation
Eating yogurt with berries from the farm
Drinking a cup of coffee, black

[5/25/21]

* * *

Now playing 10:54 a.m.
Seiji Ozawa celebrates his 85th birthday with his recording of
Beethoven's *Symphony No. 7* in A Major, Op. 92
I. Poco sostenuto – Vivace
II. Allegretto
III. Presto – Assai meno presto
IV. Allegro con brio
From the album *Beethoven: Leonore Overture No. 3; Symphony No. 7*
UMG Decca Music Group Ltd. 2020 Classical GBBBC2000162

Recorded live in 2016/2017
With Saito Kinen Orchestra

Cereal Music WKCR
May 27, 2021 9:30 a.m. – 12:00 p.m.

[5/27/21]

* * *

May 30th was my mother's 93rd birthday
She is happy, although sometimes in pain,
She is able to smile and see what is worth
Smiling about in daily life, she still makes

Connections, as when I was reading to her
The other day, and she went on a long
Monologue before concluding it was
A terrible story...

June 4th was my birthday, a nice lunch
At a remote diner, I was taken back
In time to other places, real locations
With tile floors and barstools...
Some sort of inversion though,
An inept effort on my part,
I needed and asked for another try
So we went to a basketball game last night
The Nets were playing The Bucks
It was my first playoff game ever
In any sport, incredible energy
Agility and timing

Later, Isaac and Oliver and I went
To the basement and jammed for
About an hour, and then I slept
I've been waking exhausted
For the last five or six years
This morning finally, I could sleep

[6/6/21]

* * *

Today the 17-year cicadas are going crazy!
A constant wave of sound, underpinning,
Then upward roar, an almost entheogenic
Constant rush pushing us up into trees
Where they rest, then fly about rapidly
Coursing through air to another post

Magicicada their genus and their genius
Spend 99.5% of their lives underground
As nymphs, after 17 years of surviving on
Xylem fluids, they emerge, shed their nymph

Husks, long-winged, red-eyed, built
With sturdy tympals that vibrate
In the males in chorus aggregates,
Summoning mates...

Their brief-lived adult forms are adapted
For one purpose: reproduction
Males alternate bouts of music-making
With swift flights from tree to tree
In search of a mate

Receptive females respond with timed
Wing-flicks
In addition to their congregating songs,
Males produce a distinctive courtship song
When approaching a female...

Both males and females can mate
Multiple times, but females seem to only once

After mating, females dig V-shaped grooves
In bark, depositing about 20 eggs in each
For a total of about 600

After six to 10 weeks the eggs hatch and
The nymphs fall to the ground, where they
Burrow under and begin another 17-year wait

Adults live four to six weeks, the females lay eggs
In bark, and then they die
They are remarkable, among other reasons,
Because all the members of the species
Have synchronized life cycles
No other cicada species (of about 3,000)
Does this

There are 30 different broods of periodic
Cicadas that were identified by C.L. Marlatt in 1898
The ones near here are Brood X
Magicicada septendecim

Who thrive from New York to West Virginia,
Out through Kentucky to Illinois and Michigan
We'll see them again in 2038

[6/6/21]

CANTO
DOCE

I don't want anything to end.

The ball is frozen in midair
Brooke Lopez has hurled it
From the foul line
We are enmeshed in
The playoffs as only they
Who struggle toward rest
Can be, hurtling

The ball goes in
Lopez looks intense
On the line, knowledge
That this is a game
Played at its highest level
He sinks the second

Galo sinks a three
Tucker blows a floater

[7/3/21]

* * *

I watched a poetry reading
From the safety of my avatar
I was there though really listening
Sometimes, even in person, I prefer
To listen with eyes closed, invisible

[7/4/21]

* * *

Someone once said Reggae is a kind of music
That sounds good very loud and also very low

I've learned these past days that listening
To classical music very loud is the best way

To get to know it, we really hear it for the first time
Ravel's jazz-infused *Piano Concerto in G* for example

But even Carl Maria Von Weber, whom I always
Disregarded, has something to say today

As does Amy Marcy Cheney Beach, in her
Arctic Night from *Four Eskimo Pieces*

[7/19/21]

* * *

We are out in the country, living a daily life
Listening to the radio, cooking something to eat
Doing some meditation, tai chi, and yoga
And here is, maybe, the end of the long poem
But then again, maybe not, we've thought
It could end but then wanted it to continue
As the feeling of having it continue is so
Pleasurable, so today we don't have to decide

From Purses To Paintings To Puppets
Says the headline of an article about
Sophie Taeuber-Arp, who, they say,
Blurred the line between fine and
Applied art, a watercolor on paper
From 1918, a wool cushion from
Around 1922, a pencil work from
1941, her bags the trend for today

Michael Conforto, two doubles Saturday,
A home run yesterday, a home run today,
And all of a sudden, things are looking brighter

The Mets are starting to become
One of those teams that travels,
If you know what I mean,
The Cubs do that, The Red Sox do that,
Certainly The Yankees, The Dodgers,
Teams that, when they get on the road,
They always have a lot of fans

You gotta wonder what Conforto
And Alonso are jawing, all smiles

Musicians Speak Up for Creative Equity
Struggling artists are questioning
The economics of streaming,
Which rewards stars

Rachel Kushner remembers
Silver sluggers and gold gloves
"Sometimes I'm boggled by
The gallery of souls I've known,
The lore, the wild history unsung"

* * *

I've stopped at the perfect frame:
New York Mets at Cincinnati Reds
Bottom of the 2nd, Reds already ahead
6-3, Tyler Naquin pulls one long but foul
It's caught by a guy seated up with his
Partner in baseball, his woman
I've stopped them mid-moment,
Midsummer, July 19, mid-game,
Both in Reds red, his T sports a big C
Hers the classic tag "CINCY"
He's got the ball in his right hand
Points, gesturing, while his left
Cradles his soda, sunglasses perched
On his short hair, he's talking to
Someone a row behind, over
A few, one row in front of
The mesh barrier, she looks in the
Same direction, left arm on armrest
Right hand on her right knee, crossed
Over her left, she's got a ring in
Her ear, her hair's piled high

If we were to talk, we might not agree
Politically, but can we put that aside
For a moment, and just agree that
This is cool, two people who like
Each other, sitting alone in the hot
Night, in T-shirts, enjoying the game
And the serendipity of an actual game
Ball that has landed in their lap?

[7/19/21]

* * *

The birds have quieted down
They've done their evening song
There's still light in the sky
But they've gone to sleep
And the crickets have begun

[7/19/21]

* * *

Another day
Mikhail Glinka on the box
His *Waltz Fantasy in B Minor*
Originally written for piano in 1839
It was orchestrated in 1845
But that was lost
It was re-orchestrated in 1856

There is in it
That ache of change
And also a hypnotic
Repetition

[7/20/21]

* * *

if anything ends I'll have to leave
Princess di Sigaldi of Monaco and her bronze father
with his arms in the air in a bikini at the harbor entrance before
the Monte Carlo Casino James Bond is about to enter
and I have to leave Emma Goldman writing her memoirs
to Peggy Guggenheim in St. Tropez where Gloria Soler Cera
went in search of her and reported in Catalan
that she had found the famous anarchist's cottage
at 19 Chemin de St. Antoine where the Bon Esprit house
now sits unmentioned by travel guides
and if anything ends I'll have to leave the unemployed
German travel guide at breakfast in St. Jean Cap Ferrat
who found from her historian friend in Frankfurt via email
Gloria Soler Cera's journal and put it for us in Google English.
If anything ends I cannot pose the central question of whether
Peggy Guggenheim driving her coked-up drunk friends at 3 a.m.
to wake up her famous anarchist to do a little "anarchism"
was more harmful to her memoirs than the censorship of Emma's story
by the Anarchist International.
If anything ends we must leave out France.
A terrible fate for a country that gave us so many poets!

* * *

The
Best
Care
Possible

I've been thinking and reading
And listening to music and going
For bike rides and looking at the light
On the side of a building
I can stay out all day
And no one can really get to me
Me and my books
And my writing
That's where I'm most at home

It's a sunny day, around 82 degrees
In July, the trees look green,
The sky is blue, there are some clouds
But not enough for worry

I wonder how Yvonne is doing
Up in Maine, it was great
To be able to see her earlier this summer

* * *

I don't want anything to end

BLACK WIDOW PRESS MODERN POETS

All the Good Hiding Places by Ralph Adamo

ABCs of Translation by Willis Barnstone

The Secret Brain: Selected Poems 1995-2012 by Dave Brinks

Caveat Onus: The Complete Poem Cycle by Dave Brinks

No Time for Nightmares by Andrei Codrescu

Forgiven Submarine by Andrei Codrescu and Ruxandra Cesereanu

Crusader Woman by Ruxandra Cesereanu

California (on the Somes) by Ruxandra Cesereanu. translated by Adam Sorkin.

Anticline by Clayton Eshleman

Archaic Design by Clayton Eshleman

Alchemist With One Eye on Fire by Clayton Eshleman

The Price of Experience by Clayton Eshleman

Pollen Aria by Clayton Eshleman

The Essential Poetry (1960 to 2015) by Clayton Eshleman

Grindstone of Rapport: A Clayton Eshleman Reader by Clayton Eshleman

Penetralia by Clayton Eshleman

Clayton Eshleman: The Whole Art edited by Stuart Kendall

Barzakh (Poems 2000-2012) by Pierre Joris

Packing Light: New & Selected Poems by Marilyn Kallet

How Our Bodies Learned by Marilyn Kallet

The Love That Moves Me by Marilyn Kallet

The Hexagon by Robert Kelly

Fire Exit by Robert Kelly

Garage Elegies by Stephen Kessler

Last Call by Stephen Kessler

Memory Wing by Bill Lavender

From Stone This Running by Heller Levinson

Un by Heller Levinson

Wrack Lariat by Heller Levinson

Linguaquake by Heller Levinson

Tenebraed by Heller Levinson

Seep by Heller Levinson

Lurk by Heller Levinson

LURE Heller Levinson

Shift Gristle by Heller Levinson

Query Caboodle Heller Levinson

jus' sayin' by Heller Levinson

Dada Budapest by John Olson

Backscatter by John Olson

Larynx Galaxy by John Olson

Weave Of the Dream King by John Olson

City Without People: The Katrina Poems by Niyi Osundare

Green: Sighs of An Ailing Planet by Niyi Osundare

An American Unconscious by Mebane Robertson

Signal From Draco: New & Selected Poems by Mebane Robertson

President of Desolation & Other Poems by Jerome Rothenberg

Barbaric Vast & Wild: An Assemblage of Outside & Subterranean Poetry from Origins to Present. Edited by Jerome Rothenberg and John Bloomberg-Rissman

Concealments and Caprichos by Jerome Rothenberg

Eye of Witness: a Jerome Rothenberg Reader. Edited by Heribeto Yepez and jerome rothenberg

Soraya by Anis Shivani

Fractal Song by Jerry W. Ward, Jr.

Beginnings of the Prose Poem. Edited by Mary Ann Caws and Michel Delville

BLACK WIDOW PRESS POETRY IN TRANSLATION

The Great Madness. by Avigdor Hameiri. Translated and edited by Peter C. Appelbaum

Of Human Carnage - Odessa 1918-1920. by Avigdor Hameiri. Translated and edited by Peter C. Appelbaum. Introduction by Dan Hecht

Howls & Growls: French Poems to Bark By. Translated by Norman R. Shapiro & Illustrated by Olga Pastuchiv

A Flea the Size of Paris: The Old French "Fatrasies" and "Fatras". Translated by Ted Byrne and Donato Mancini

In Praise of Sleep: Selected Poems of Lucian Blaga. by Lucian Blaga. Translated by Andrei Codrescu

Rhymamusings. by Pierre Coran. Translated by Norman R. Shapiro

Through Naked Branches: Selected Poems of Tarjei Vesaas by Tarjei Vesaas. Translated by Roger Greenwald

I Have Invented Nothing: Selected Poems by Jean-Pierre Rosnay. Translated by J. Kates

Fables of Town & Country by Pierre Coran. Translated by Norman R. Shapiro & Illustrated by Olga Pastuchiv

Earthlight (Clair de Terre): Poems by André Breton. Translated by Bill Zavatsky and Zack Rogow

The Gentle Genius of Cecile Perin: Selected Poems (1906-1956) by Cecile Perin. Translated by Norman R. Shapiro

Boris Vian Invents Boris Vian: a Boris Vian Reader by Boris Vian. Edited and Translated by Julia Older with a Preface by Patrick Vian

Forbidden Pleasures: New Selected Poems [1924-1949] by Luis Cernuda. Translated by Stephen Kessler

Fables in a Modern Key (fables dans l'air du temps) by Pierre Coran. Translated by Norman R. Shapiro & Illustrated by Olga Pastuchiv

Exile Is My Trade: A Habib Tengour Reader by Habib Tengour. Translated by Pierre Joris

Present Tense of the World: Poems 2000-2009 by Amina Said. Translated by Marilyn Hacker

Endure: Poems by Bei Dao. Translated by Clayton Eshleman and Lucas Klein

Curdled Skulls: Poems of Bernard Bador by Bernard Bador. Co-translated and edited by Clayton Eshleman

Pierre Reverdy: Poems Early to Late by Pierre Reverdy. Translated by Mary Ann Caws and Patricia Terry

Selected Prose and Poetry of Jules Supervielle by Jules Supervielle. Translated by Nancy Kline, Patrica Terry, and Kathleen Micklow

Poems of Consummation by Vicente Aleixandre. Translated by Stephen Kessler

A Life of Poems, Poems of a Life by Anna de Noailles. Translated by Norman R. Shapiro

Furor & Mystery and Other Poems by Rene Char. Translated by Mary Ann Caws and Nancy Kline

The Big Game (Le grand jeu) by Benjamin Péret. Translated by Marilyn Kallet

Essential Poems & Prose of Jules Laforgue by Jules Laforgue. Translated by Patricia Terry

Preversities: A Jacques Prevert Sampler by Jacques Prevert. Translated by Norman R. Shapiro

La Fontaine's Bawdy by Jean de la Fontaine. Translated by Norman R. Shapiro & Illustrated by David Schorr

BLACK WIDOW PRESS BIOGRAPHY

www.blackwidowpress.com